A Bite-Sized Publi

C000099976

We Don't Believe You

Why Populists and the Establishment See the World Differently

John Redwood

Published by Bite-Sized Books Ltd 2019

Bite-Sized Books Ltd Cleeve Croft, Cleeve Road, Goring RG8 9BJ UK
information@bite-sizedbooks.com
Registered in the UK. Company Registration No: 9395379

Bite-Sized Books Ltd Cleeve Croft, Cleeve Road, Goring RG8 9BJ UK
information@bite-sizedbooks.com
Registered in the UK. Company Registration No: 9395379
ISBN: 9781095254950

Contents

Sir John Redwood MP

John Redwood is a leading commentator on world economies. The author of books on the Euro, popular capitalism, the global marketplace and the credit crunch, he sets out in this exciting new analysis the impact of austerity economics and the banking crash on societies and governments around the world. He is a Distinguished Fellow of All Souls College Oxford, a regular contributor to newspapers and the media, and a frequent lecturer on economic topics.

He brings to this book the past experience of leading a couple of international manufacturing businesses and his work as a financial innovator. He was an early advocate and expert on privatisation and third way financing of public services, and set up an investment business to pioneer dynamic passive investing. He has been a Professor at Middlesex University Business School.

He attempts in the book to look at the role of experts, who are themselves often on the wrong end of populist criticism. He concludes with the establishment that expertise is a good thing when genuine and well used, but agrees with the populists that some consensus expertise on economics in recent years has peddled dangerous doctrines and false forecasts to the detriment of our well-being.

He sees the populist revolt extending further, unless the establishments adjust their scripts and seek to understand better the forces they have unwittingly unleashed. Why didn't they foresee the banking crash? How could they not understand the rise of Mr Trump? Why were they taken aback by the hostility to austerity economics? He himself predicted the economic damage done by the European Exchange Rate Mechanism and forecast the market meltdown from the banking crash.

He is the Conservative MP for Wokingham. He was formerly Secretary of State for Wales in John Major's Cabinet, and twice a candidate for the leadership of the Conservative Party in the 1990s.

The new vs the familiar

Populism is on the march. On both sides of the Atlantic the traditional parties of the centre left and centre right are being assailed by new populist movements, or being taken over by populist candidates.

In the USA and the UK the old parties survive by changing. Donald Trump emerged as the unlikely Republican President despite every attempt of the party grandees to stop him running. Hilary Clinton's establishment campaign was almost derailed by a challenge from the left. Jeremy Corbyn leads the UK Labour party in a new radical socialist direction, whilst the UK Conservatives have adopted leaving the EU in order to try to reunite with their voters.

On the European continent the second half of the twentieth century saw a pattern of government alternating between Christian Democrats and Social Democrats.

The differences of policy were contained by a general reverence for the bureaucratic establishment and a pragmatic understanding of what was "possible" in government. They all bought into ever closer union and the Euro scheme which meant lifting economic policy out of national democratic debate.

The conservatives wanted a bit less government, and a bit lower taxes. The socialists wanted a bit more government and bit more public spending. This happy alternation with limited change has been disrupted or swept away in every country.

In Greece a left-wing challenger party against the Euro destroyed the power cartel of Pasok and New Democracy. In Italy the Christian Democrats were first overwhelmed by the populism of Forza. Later both Forza itself and the Socialists were swept aside by Five Star and Lega preaching against the European based consensus on economic policy.

France held a Presidential election where neither the republicans nor the socialists, the traditional parties of power, had a candidate in the last two. An entirely new force, En Marche, faced the National Front.

In Germany, the long term winner from the Euro, the Christian Democrats and the Social Democrats, the old rivals, have to govern in grand coalition together to keep out the insurgent Greens and the AFD, an anti-Euro party which wants new controls on migration. Mrs Merkel can no longer command her own party so she has announced her eventual retirement. The two traditional dominant parties cannot command even half of the vote together.

Healthy scepticism

It has always been the case that democracies thrive on a healthy scepticism about rulers and governments. Differing views and strong debates are not new. Anti-clericalism is an old phenomenon which has morphed into a disdain for some of the experts and some of their claims.

What is new in this democratic era is the intensity of the scorn for those who want to see the old party system and the current range of governing institutions continue as they are.

There is a growing wish to force change through the ballot box, on the social media and through the general public debate and commentary of where we are now.

The elites feel uncomfortable. Rumours race round the world about them at a press of a mobile phone screen. Investigators and critics unearth their made up or real crimes. Feeling the need to communicate, more members of the elite often just expose themselves to more abuse and criticism by tweeting or using the media.

The establishments have been jolted by people voting the wrong way as they see it.

In Brazil a socialist establishment found it difficult to accept the election of a right wing populist with opinions they found offensive. Half of the USA including much of the establishment wrestles with Mr Trump's abrasive style, whilst his substantial support base loves his more extreme comments as "telling it as it is".

Half of the UK is excited at the thought of casting off the bureaucracy and legal rules of Brussels, whilst a core of the establishment believes it will be "catastrophic". Many Germans worry about the AFD getting closer to power, whilst the AFD's growing fan base see them as the necessary antidote to a Berlin elite who have ignored their wishes on migration, energy and much else.

This book will ask why is this happening now? How should we explain the simultaneous eruption of such frustration over the way we are governed in democracies?

Why have so many traditional parties failed to adjust to the new mood, and opted instead for decline or political death beneath the juggernaut of populist parties? Why do some of these parties come from the so called left, and some from the so called right? Do they have much in common?

We will explore how the economies of the west were damaged by the banking crash and by the Euro scheme, leaving the experts at a loss to explain how they could have got it so wrong.

People feel they were punished for the errors of the elite, whilst the central bankers stayed in office and the commercial bankers kept their bonuses.

We will travel into countries with nationalist movements and with campaigns for regional independence, questioning why identity has become so dominant an issue.

In a time of rapid technical change many seem to want old certainties based on place and culture, and dislike the elite's seeming carelessness about tradition and social cohesion.

In one sense the populists movements are a huge attempt to wrestle power back, to get it back from seemingly unaccountable so called independent bodies, and from political parties that lie or let people down. There is a very strong feeling that too many top politicians, executives and quango heads are in it for what they can get out of rather than for what they can do to serve.

In law and order many feel especially let down. They dislike violence on the streets, fear for theft and burglary against their property, are amazed at the incidence of cyber crime, and seek to attribute causes that are rooted in the very policies they see the elite pursuing.

Populists often feel the authorities are more concerned about thought crime than physical crime, and worry that crimes of all kinds are used as an excuse by what they call the deep state to gain ever more control over their data and their lives. People both want the freedoms new technology can bring them to improve their lives, and protection from the state using it to tax and regulate them more.

The media are part of the story. The huge changes underway in how we see and hear news, how we send messages, how we shop and how we communicate is causing a revolution in the conventional media.

People are increasingly resistant to the top down editorial control of the news and the message from traditional tv and newspapers, as they become their own reporters and editors with direct access to the web and social media.

The opportunity of the digital revolution

Fake news is now a charge against the establishment, who are thought to control and corrupt the news and message serving their own ends. It is also a counter charge by the established media, who remind the populists that they observe standards of accuracy in reporting, of some decorum in language and accept the law of libel, which may be less observed in the wild fringes of social media.

The digital revolution is exciting, full of opportunity. It is upending old business models, and bringing to many people something new that they want.

It gives shoppers more choice, more convenience and lower prices. It brings entertainment and comment in many more forms available when we want it, not just when a main channel schedules it. It allows more direct democracy with instant polls and surveys, more access to those making decisions, and more transparency of what they are doing. It also destroys old jobs and old businesses, and worries more people about their futures.

Governments and political parties that cannot ride this tiger well will perish. They need both to embrace the best of the new, and avoid cutting themselves off from the familiar and traditional in ways which alienate many voters.

Chapter 1

Austerity is an elite doctrine that the right and left hate

Voters don't believe governments that wage austerity on the unwilling. Mainly they think such policies are either needless or self-defeating

Populist movements around the world are on the rise. Many more people are saying to the experts and the elites who would continue to govern them, "We don't believe you". The Emperors have no clothes. They have cried wolf too often on worries they have for the public to trust them.

Worse still, their fabled expertise has so often led their countries and the world system into trouble. If you look for a single issue which did more than others to fuel the distrust and to fan the flames of radical politics, it is the failure of the economic elite to foresee crashes and crises.

Over the last ten years real incomes have fallen in several advanced countries and risen slowly elsewhere. The public feels let down by the experts and expects them to help deliver faster and better progress to higher living standards.

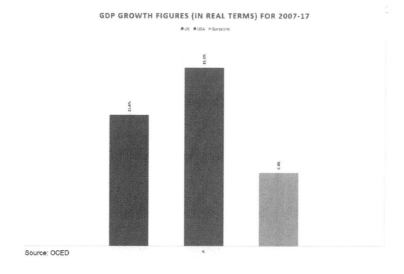

GDP GROWTH FIGURES (IN REAL TERMS) FOR 2007-17

Source: OCED

The biggest western failure was the complacency about banks and banking throughout the first seven years of this century. It was followed by a spectacular crash and great recession, engineered by the very governments and Central banks who had presided over the credit bubble.

They failed to alert people to its dangers and then brought the banks crashing down as if it had nothing to do with them. As the Queen asked in the UK, why didn't the experts see it coming?

Of course, in practice some experts did, but we were marginalised, excluded from positions of power by the great consensus. The false expertise of the establishment blandly told us this time it would be different. The experts in authority told us that banks were now large and global. They had better ways of managing risk. It was therefore just fine for these global banks to have so much less cash and capital relative to the business they wrote than had been fashionable in the previous century.

The advent of more derivatives, options, securitised loans and big capital markets meant we need not worry. The leading banks would use these devices to offset risk. They would not be stretched if large numbers of depositors wanted their money back at the same time. There was according to the elite no reason for that to happen.

The experts were wrong

We now know that they were wrong. The heavily leveraged positions in options and derivatives meant some investment funds and institutions were dangerously over committed and vulnerable to any downturn. Instead of using new vehicles to offset they risk they often used them to raise it to increase profits in good times.

Worse still, having created a system that built up huge debt mountains backed by modest sums of cash and capital, the authorities then proceeded to blame the banks and to bring them down for having inadequate balance sheets.

The regulators acted as if they had been unaware of what was happening. They undermined a system which could have been deflated more gently with less public worry from highlighting its failings. The public denunciation of the banks by regulators encouraged depositors to queue to get their money back in a hurry.

Many people now recognise the big error made in allowing far too many loans to be made without the banks making proper provision for losses. Fewer commentators to this day see in some ways the larger error. Having allowed easier terms, the central banks and governments suddenly changed their mind. They rushed into expecting banks to hold large additional sums of capital which they found difficult to raise against the background of alarms set off by their regulators. Pointing out the frailties created made the crisis more immediate and more dramatic.

The public was fairly willing to blame the commercial bank executives, and to go along with the establishment view that this was primarily a private sector banking error.

Pursuing cases against banks and bankers for mis-selling, for running too much risk, for manipulating markets and the rest was a popular sport. The public egged on the authorities, and if anything felt too few bankers were fined or imprisoned for all the excesses that occurred.

There was no similar wish to pillory the central bankers who had allowed these extreme behaviours and had acted as apologists. They had shared the view that these extra risks were fine owing to the global nature of the big banks and their superior risk management with a wide range of so called risk reducing instruments to hand.

The establishment decided if it cut loose the commercial bankers and blamed them, it would survive itself. Reading many of the commentators and newspapers of the time, it seemed they got away with it.

In practice the establishment was badly damaged and seen to be generally responsible for the disaster. Voters took delight in getting rid of incumbent governments who had presided over the crash.

In the USA the Presidency switched from Republican to Democrat during the worst period of the crisis. In the UK the long-lived Labour government was swept from power at the first general election to follow the recession.

On the continent where the crisis took longer to come through but was worse and more prolonged thanks to the Euro, government after government fell, as we will see later in this story.

Something else gave as well. The reputation of experts and large economic institutions like the IMF, World Bank, national central banks and treasuries also suffered long-term damage. None had forecast the collapse. None had taken early action to cushion or avoid the collapse.

Why should we believe their next set of forecasts when they simply were unable to forecast the great recession even a few months before it hit?

Their reputations were to suffer more and for longer because of the way they handled the aftermath of the crisis. Instead of doing everything to cushion the blow and then to speed the recovery, they opted instead for a series of policies that were soon called austerity.

In the UK the authorities switched from defending the build-up of credit and derivatives, to stating that it had gone too far and the commercial banks were to blame. They told them to rein in their balance sheets, cut down their loan books and raise more cash and capital in a hurry.

The Governor of the Bank of England told them it was not the central bank's task to bail them out, and they had to pay the price for their own moral hazard.

The first major casualty was Northern Rock, a mortgage bank that had expanded rapidly in the previous few years. The general words of the regulators led to a sharp loss of confidence in the bank with too many depositors wanting to withdraw their money.

The collapse led to a reconstruction, with the authorities changing their stance and putting money into markets to try to ease the squeeze. It was difficult to see what was gained by allowing the collapse of a bank that was in the early days illiquid rather than insolvent. Forcing early disposals of loans helped make it insolvent.

Triggering the recession which duly followed the banking crash then turned many of the good loans into bad loans for various banks intensifying the squeeze further.

The Northern Rock business model entailed lending on mortgage for house purchase. The bank then sold on some of the loans to other market participants so the bank could carry on expanding the mortgage portfolio.

Securitising or selling on loans was a strong part of the model, taking risk off Northern Rock's balance sheet and allowing it to expand mortgage business further.

Once this was questioned by the regulator it became more difficult for the Bank to sell the mortgages on for a profit, leaving it exposed to rumours and worries about its solvency.

The Bank of England as lender of last resort to the commercial banks could have made enough cash available to Northern Rock to carry on, but chose not to. Many commentators argued that securitising the loans was the cause of the problem. Securitising was part of the answer to the problem, as it generated cash for Northern Rock and transferred the risk to others.

What brought the bank down was the inability to borrow enough short term money at an affordable price in a market starved of cash and gripped by fear partly driven by regulatory comment and actions. This led directly to a run on the bank by depositors who were the people who forced action to save the bank.

The unlearned lessons

The establishment did not learn from the bitter experience of Northern Rock. They did end up putting plenty of cash into the system to prevent the complete collapse of the bank, but only after the run on deposits and the forced recapitalisation.

Instead of learning that earlier support coupled with a planned programme to strengthen the balance sheet would have avoided a lot of pain and cost, they did exactly the same to the much bigger RBS, intensifying the crisis a year later when a run started to emerge on RBS deposits.

Taxpayers ended up having to underwrite and partially pay for a very expensive bail out of some of the leading commercial banks, which added to public anger about what had happened. When RBS was given state capital it had a balance sheet valued at £2.2 trillion. That was more than the GDP of the entire UK that year. It was almost too big for the UK state to accept as a risk. A loss of just 2% of the assets meant the taxpayer would lose the equivalent of the entire defence budget for a year.

These figures did not stop an establishment in panic accepting such risks, despite other ways of handling the crisis being offered to them.

Worse was to follow. The mood of the authorities on both sides of the Atlantic shifted to a hostile approach to more borrowing. In the UK the new coalition government formed from the Conservatives and Liberal

Democrats after the 2010 election, determined that the public sector deficit had to come down.

At the same time the main commercial banks were told by the regulators to boost the ratio between capital and loans they had made, typically doubling it. In recessionary conditions banks were more inclined to do this by cutting back on loans than by raising more capital. So, austerity was born.

Car and mortgage loans were scarce, companies that wanted to borrow found it difficult, and the gap between public spending and tax revenue had to be altered dramatically from the unsustainable 10% of GDP back down below the EU ceiling of 3%.

The halving of RBS

RBS itself, the largest of the state supported banks, embarked on a massive balance sheet squeeze, halving the size of its assets and liabilities. It is amazing the UK economy did not do less well than it did, given the impact such a large reduction in credit would normally have on a captive economy.

The new Chancellor, George Osborne, was an enthusiast for the new puritanism. He told us that the UK government deficit had to be eliminated over the lifetime of a Parliament, and said he would do this primarily by reining in public spending, with just 20% of the work done by the tax rises he proposed. This seemed an unlikely approach at the time given the pressures on spending and the spending proclivities of most politicians.

So, began a long argument I had with the Treasury over what the true figures were.

Whilst the Chancellor and the Treasury documents told us the bulk of the adjustment came from spending cuts, the official figures published in the Budget books showed a totally different picture. They showed that the plan was for a very small real increase in total public spending over the forecast period, with cash spending going up all the time to take care of inflation.

The deficit came down thanks to a massive increase in tax revenues. Tax revenues did expand thanks to modest economic growth and to the increase in the VAT rate, but not sufficiently to achieve the stated objective of eliminating the deficit altogether.

The gap between the rhetoric and the reality was damaging. Whilst some spending programmes were cut, the continued growth of overseas aid, EU contributions, NHS and benefit expenditure in total maintained modest growth in real spending.

People however believed the words of the government, as it married with their personal observations of the programmes which were cut.

As always, the media and the opposition understandably concentrated on where the cuts were sharpest, so hardly anyone was pointing out that total spending was still rising.

Meanwhile the substantial increase in the tax burden placed an obstacle to growth. Enterprise was held back by high rates of Income Tax, Stamp Duty, Capital Gains and other taxes on enterprise. Some tax rates were clearly counterproductive leading to less being raised than if they had been lower.

After long debate the Chancellor did cut the top rate of Income tax from the penal 50% introduced as a poison pill at the very end of Labour's period in office, and as expected revenue increased substantially.

All of this gave austerity a bad name. The opposition both criticised it as a bad policy for those who suffered from the cuts, and criticised the government for failing to get additional borrowing down as planned. The Chancellor was especially keen to cut benefit spending.

It is true that you can cut benefit spending by promoting growth, more jobs and higher pay. If benefit spending falls off because fewer people need the benefits that is a good outcome. He also, however, decided to cut benefits for some who did need them.

Caps were popular

Putting an overall cap on how much total benefit a person or family could receive turned out to be a popular policy. Many felt it was wrong that someone not at work could pick up more net pay in benefits than someone on average earnings could earn after tax.

The decision to reduce payments for housing to those who lived in rented accommodation on benefits who rented a home larger than they strictly needed was more contentious. Dubbed the bedroom tax by Labour, it became an image of a cut too far for many. Someone in need of benefits did not want to feel they had to move to a smaller place at the same time as losing their job or hitting some other financial accident.

Austerity in the UK came to mean for the rest of the community restrictions on pay awards, high levels of taxation, and a lack of progress in raising net incomes over a prolonged period.

It is true for much of the time after 2010 real incomes were rising a little, but the drop-in take home pay and disposable income during the crash years of 2008-9 had been large and it took time to recover.

Where many politicians saw austerity as primarily a public-sector phenomenon with a knock-on effect to those dependent on benefits and public services, many others saw it as their own experience as they reflected on the decline in living standards brought on by the crash and slow progress in recovery. It took until 2015 for UK incomes on average to be above the real levels of 2007.

The European experiences

Austerity was altogether much fiercer in parts of the Eurozone. In the case of Greece, the austerity was both reflected in huge cuts in cash spending by government, and by a big squeeze in real incomes for most others. The two interacted, as successive budgets cut cash pay for public sector workers by as much as one fifth, and cut pensions payable to the retired. In addition, tax increases were put through.

Greek living standards fell by a staggering one third and remain today well below 2007 levels. The programmes of cuts and tax rises were continuous through the last eight years as the masters of the Euro and the EU forced Greece into successive austerity budgets.

The opposition to this was active and continuous, mainly using Parliamentary means. The public expressed their feelings in elections, striking out governing parties for their failure to find a way out of austerity.

In the end, however, they reluctantly accepted the Euro scheme which depended on the austerity treatment. Italy had a less dramatic version of the same experiences. A country loaded with debt prior to the crash of 2008-9, the government had to accept regular budgets that pushed down on spending and increased taxes to try to bridge the gap between revenue and outgoings. The Italian economy grew very slowly, forcing more action on tax and spending to try to right the accounts.

The debates about austerity economics still rage.

The establishment say that austerity is a necessary discipline. They argue a country like a household or a business cannot borrow its way out of debt, and cannot borrow its way to faster growth. They argue that where a country like Ireland took the harsh medicine it was able subsequently to recover faster.

The problem with the Irish example is the way the Irish government kept corporate taxes far lower than most of the rest of the EU, which successfully attracted more business and capital. This met with disapproval by the EU, but not to the point where they prevented it happening. It was a model that the EU could just about tolerate for a small country, but would have been altogether more challenging if an Italy or Spain had tried it.

The critics of austerity make various arguments. They point out that success as in the cases of the UK and Ireland in getting the deficit down whilst also growing owes a lot to setting lower tax rates, not higher ones. The austerity plans of the EU usually require higher tax rates. They argue that borrowing more to invest and grow may succeed in cutting debt later, as deficits are very sensitive to rates of growth of the supporting economy.

The Italian and Greek deficits have proved intractable partly because their GDP has been static or falling, reducing the amount of tax revenue raised and increasing the strains on public spending particularly for benefits. If growth had been faster benefit spending would have been lower and tax revenue naturally more buoyant.

The Italian budget deficit argument in 2018 was about just this issue. The coalition government argued that spending more and taxing less would reduce the deficit faster in later years, whilst the EU concentrated on the immediate impact which was to make the deficit larger.

Rising tensions

All of these arguments increased the tension between those who govern and those who have to live with their taxes and spending plans. It sometimes appeared as if the governing class took some pleasure in announcing more austerity.

When attention then passed to examining their lifestyles, they did not always seem to apply the same prudence or puritanism to their own lives.

On both sides of the Atlantic there was more intense scrutiny of perks and expenses claimed by the elites of the public sector, and more questions asked about the extent of their travel, their overnight stays, their conference going and their bonuses. It made it worse if the recipient of generous total remuneration and expenses was lecturing everyone else on the need to keep pay and benefits down.

There are limits to how much austerity people living in a democracy will stand. They need to be persuaded that there is a good reason for it, that it will end, and that there will be a better future at some point.

People will accept much more privation in a war when they agree their country has to fight for its survival and for its principles, as with the allies in 1939-45 against their Axis opponents.

They will accept the need to right the mess created by a banking crash and recession, but will be more sceptical if the same establishment that landed them in the mess seeks to get them out of it.

When governments change

It is true there is usually government change following such a crisis, as there was on both sides of the Atlantic after the crash of 2008. This helps create a willingness to follow a new lead. The danger is, however, that the leaders of the central bank, the commercial banks, the treasury and the other principal public sector institutions do not change their approach and show sufficient humility for past errors, which makes the task of recovery more difficult.

The UK made more rapid progress in recovery and had a more honest dialogue about past errors because it did have a clear change of government.

In the Euro area, as we will see, national governments came and went, but the overall direction and policy of the EU and the ECB carried on regardless, to the concern of the troubled countries to the south and west of the zone. There it was only the decision of the central bank to ignore German advice and to print money that prevented a far worse crisis.

When something goes badly wrong, like the banking crash, having accountable government you can sack does help emotionally as people wrestle with the damage their governing institutions have done to them.

The outcome was not worse because the authorities flipped from being austere about banks' capital and money to being accommodating through inventing Quantitative Easing.

They wished to teach the private sector and its bankers a lesson by curtailing extra credit and imposing many new restrictive rules, but they did realise that would prevent money growth and impede recovery.

So, the Fed, the Bank of England and eventually even the European Central Bank set about creating more money themselves directly.

Normally extra money results from commercial banks' lending money to people. That money is deposited back in banks by the companies and individuals that are paid it by the borrowers, so the banks can then lend some of it on again, thus multiplying money in the system.

Instead the three main central banks of the west created new money in an account as only they can, and then went out and spent it on buying up government debt. This served to raise the price of such bonds, lowering the interest rate the government had to pay for future borrowings. It also meant the former owners of the bonds had cash which they could reinvest in riskier assets or spend. In practice it meant the government spent the money created without having to pay for it.

This is not normally carried out, as in conditions where the commercial banks can create money and finance growth it would be very inflationary to simply print more money. Countries that have tried it have ended up with damagingly high rates of inflation.

Electorates sick of austerity

This time with broken and cowed commercial banks there was no unacceptable general inflation. There was however a substantial asset price inflation as highly priced bonds were swapped for highly priced shares or properties.

Austerity has been the characteristic of the last decade. Electorates are sick and tired of it. They feel there should now be some bonus or reward for past belt tightening. Individuals look around at various causes, worrying about migration and its impact on wages, at governments cutting when spending is needed, at tax rises when people want to keep more of their own money.

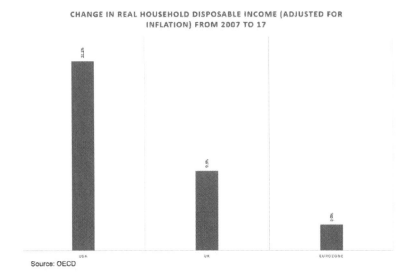

CHANGE IN REAL HOUSEHOLD DISPOSABLE INCOME (ADJUSTED FOR INFLATION) FROM 2007 TO 17

Source: OECD

These ideas fuel the radical political movements of right and left that wish to end austerity and offer something better. They say to governments who wage more austerity on unwilling voters, we don't believe you. People think their austerity policies are either needless or self-defeating.

Chapter 2

The Euro – at the core of the elite's project

A currency has been introduced without explaining the full exchange of power from national to EU level it requires. This means it is subject to scares and alarms no normal single currency faces

The Euro is the largest threat to the national democracy of the European nations the elite have dared launch. It is the quintessential elite project.

The rules of the scheme are laid down from the centre by senior officials. Any country in the Euro has to abide by the budget rules, and has to accept the general direction of its economic policy from Brussels. Individual countries still hold general elections and allow heated debate about economic policy, taxation, and spending as if they still had national choices, yet in practice there is little an elected government can do to change economic course.

Much of the recent political history of the Eurozone is the story of individual countries seeking to amend or throw off Euro discipline, only to find they are not allowed to.

The Euro has humbled most of the traditional centre right and centre left parties of the continent, throwing up new challenger parties trying to find a way round the impasse of Euro policy.

Most recently the Italians elected a coalition government of two anti-Euro parties, Lega and Cinque Stelle. The new government set out an austerity busting budget in accordance with their Manifesto promises, only to be told they had to cut back the spending and increase the taxes in order to comply with Euro rules. Such is life in the Euro for any former national democracy.

The origins of the Euro came in the last century. The crusaders for a united Europe decided a single currency would be the force that brought once fiercely independent nations together under one control. It was sold as a means of extending the single market, removing some of the costs of transactions by removing the need to change money when you exchanged goods or services.

An argument about ease of trading and transaction costs was used to front run a massive constitutional change which would have profound consequences for jobs, savings, banking and democracy itself.

The early attempts to get a single currency off the ground floundered with the collapse of the European Exchange Rate Mechanism (ERM). In the 1970s and 1980s the EU wanted to bring currencies together by encouraging common economic policies and gradually reducing the fluctuations of one European currency against another.

The ERM was a device to set bounds for the values of one European currency against another, and to act as a signal to markets that the EU Central Banks might intervene to police the narrow divergencies allowed. This could then lead to locking the rates and replacing the individual currencies by the Euro.

Where Italy and the UK failed

Italy and the UK always had divergent trends and a history of devaluation as both were a bit more inflation prone than the German core to the ERM zone. Markets detected this weakness and decided in 1992 that neither Italy nor the UK could maintain their published parity against the German currency, the Deutschemark.

Far from strengthening the system, the publication of the intervention bands for each currency allowed traders to pick off an individual currency and test out the resolve of the Central Banks to hold their chosen floor or ceiling for a currency value.

By 1992 it was clear the DM was too cheap and the lira and sterling were too dear. The German Central Bank compounded the problems of the system by indicating a reluctance to throw its resources in to trying to maintain the levels of the lira and the pound, so the system broke.

Italy and the UK left the ERM and allowed the markets to devalue their currencies. The ultra-high interest rates and austerity policies introduced to try to hold the pound up in the European system led directly to a sharp recession, with many closed factories, job losses and unemployment.

The crisis was presented as always by the EU as a crisis caused by the inflationary weaknesses of the two main economies forced out, rather than as a problem caused by the surplus inducing low inflation policies of Germany. It was of course a problem caused by both sides. Markets not only said the lira was too dear but they also said the DM was too cheap.

The UK reflected on its experiences in the ERM. Considerable damage was done to the UK economy and the UK's standing in the international financial world. In the early days in the ERM the pound had been under upwards pressure, with many traders thinking it was too cheap. This had led the Bank of England to create a lot of pounds to sell across the exchanges to foreign buyers, to seek to keep the pound down.

This process created excess cash in the UK banking system, which was duly lent on to UK borrowers. Using the conventional fractional reserve banking, UK banks could effectively lend an extra £10 for every pound of additional cash in their accounts.

When a foreign investor or trader bought a pound from the UK because they thought it was going up, it was likely to end up in the UK banking system to lend on. As a result, the UK had a credit fuelled bubble, with an increase in price inflation. This in turn worried markets, and led to a sharp reversal of sentiment and to the selling pressure against the pound which eventually forced the UK out of the mechanism.

The UK had an early taste of the boom-bust tendencies that first the ERM and subsequently the Euro itself generated within the member states.

Unable to leave the Euro

When I took my books and ideas against the UK joining the Euro on the road to UK voters and businesses in the 1990s, one of the most powerful arguments I could deploy was the Euro is an exchange rate mechanism you cannot get out of. Just as with the ERM, membership of the Euro is likely to cause boom and bust. UK business and voters, shaken by their harsh experiences in the ERM and by the recession it caused at the end of our brief time in it, rightly fought shy of another dose of the same treatment. They indicated in opinion poll after opinion poll they would not join the Euro.

There was no such movement against the Euro in many continental countries, and much more willingness to ignore the warnings of the ERM and to plunge onwards to full monetary union.

The Euro was established in January 1999 in parallel with national currencies. It went live as the official currency of the participating states on 1 January 2002, when large quantities of Euro notes and coins were issued.

The opening results for economies like Spain and Ireland seemed particularly favourable. The European Central Bank set one short-term interest rate for all the countries involved. The rate set in the early days was too low for some countries, which immediately went on a spending spree fuelled by cheap credit. Ireland and Spain in particular saw huge increases in property development and speculation, creating big bubbles in construction and property.

Many countries saw rapid expansion of their banking systems, taking advantage of access to large pools of money at low rates of interest. Cyprus and Ireland in particular grew banking sectors that were huge in relation to the size of the domestic economy and tax base.

The founding fathers of the Euro – and they were men – had understood some of the risks in what they were running. They therefore had laid down criteria countries had to meet before joining the currency.

Each state was meant to have kept its own national currency in line with the main currencies of the zone or with the Euro after its introduction to show similar discipline and characteristics.

No state joining was meant to have borrowed more than 60% of GDP, and each one was told to keep its budget deficit down below 3% of GDP in any given budget year. Inflation too had to be closely linked to the performance of other countries in the zone.

Rules were not followed

If these rules had all been followed the Euro would have been much more stable. The criteria looked as if they were chosen to allow Germany and a core of northern states that followed similar financial disciplines to join, whilst keeping out the high borrowing states of the south like Greece and Italy.

Unfortunately, by the turn of the century, when it fell to evaluate which countries should be allowed in to the Euro only Luxembourg actually met all the requirements. Even Germany fell foul of her own rules.

The merger of the two Germanies had given the enlarged Germany a substantially bigger state debt, so not even she qualified. As a result with

Table 8 Economic indicators and the Maastrict Treaty convergence criteria (*excluding the exchange-rate criterion*)

		Inflation (%)	Long-term interest rate (%)	General gov. lending (+) or borrowing(–) % of GDP	General gov. gross debt, % of GDP
Belgium	1995	1.4	7.5	–4.1	133.7
	1996	1.6	6.7	–3.3	130.6
Denmark	1995	2.3	8.3	–1.6	71.9
	1996	2.2	7.4	–1.4	70.2
Germany	1995	1.5	6.9	–3.5	58.1
	1996	1.3	6.3	–4.0	60.8
Greece	1995	9.0	17.4	–9.1	111.8
	1996	8.4	15.1	–7.9	110.6
Spain	1995	4.7	11.3	–6.6	65.7
	1996	3.8	9.5	–4.4	67.8
France	1995	1.7	7.5	–4.8	52.8
	1996	2.1	6.6	–4.0	56.4
Ireland	1995	2.4	8.3	–2.0	81.6
	1996	2.1	7.5	–1.6	74.7
Italy	1995	5.4	12.2	–7.1	124.9
	1996	4.7	10.3	–6.6	123.4
Luxembourg	1995	1.9	7.6	1.5	6.0
	1996	1.3	7.0	0.9	7.8
Netherlands	1995	1.1	6.9	–4.0	79.7
	1996	1.2	6.3	–2.6	78.7
Austria	1995	2.0	7.1	–5.9	69.0
	1996	1.7	6.5	–4.3	71.1
Portugal	1995	3.8	11.5	–5.1	71.7
	1996	3.0	9.4	–4.0	71.7
Finland	1995	1.0	8.8	–5.2	59.2
	1996	0.9	7.4	–3.3	61.3
Sweden	1995	2.9	10.2	–8.1	78.7
	1996	1.6	8.5	–3.9	78.1
UK	1995	3.1	8.3	–5.8	54.1
	1996	3.0	8.0	–4.6	56.3

Source: Our Currency, Our Country: The Dangers of European Monetary Union by John Redwood (1997), p175.

the Euro officials in a hurry to take this huge step towards centralised EU government, compromise was in the air.

In the end they decided that nearly all could join, however uncompliant they were. Whilst Greece did not make the first cut, as her divergence was particularly marked, in 2001 she was also allowed in with the others.

It meant that countries that had state borrowing more than twice the permitted levels, countries with a long history of devaluing against the DM and countries with persistently higher inflation were all part of the new zone. The politicians committed to the ideal of European government made decisions which the officials proposed to override the sensible rules of the scheme drafted in different times.

A gift to France

The Euro is quite unlike any other single currency. It was a gift from Germany to France to reassure France following the merger of East and West Germany.

Conscious that this made Germany considerably larger and potentially more powerful than France, the French decided they needed some proof that Germany was committed to the idea of European integration powered by a close working relationship between France and Germany.

France saw the currency as a way of harnessing Germany money and limiting independent German economic power. Germany was reluctant to sacrifice one of the great achievements of the post war West German state.

With a troubled history of hyperinflation and monetary insecurity in the inter war years of the last century, Germany after 1945 created a strong and much trusted currency with dependably low inflation. Germany agreed to her ally's request only with extreme strings attached.

Germany insisted that there would be no bail outs of states or banking systems within the zone using German money. Germany would share a currency with Italy or Greece, but would not undertake to pay the bills if things went wrong.

In a normal single currency area like the dollar or sterling, the single currency is backed up not just by a single central bank but by a single government and by access to the whole tax revenues of that state.

If economic policy fails to deliver then both the government and the central bank can take concerted action to put things right. If the central bank follows bad policies the government can instruct it to change. If one part of a single currency zone struggles to generate jobs or raise living standards within the zone it becomes a matter of grave concern to the government of that state.

As the region cannot devalue to price itself back into work, the government of the state usually mobilises subsidies, benefit payments, location of business policies and much else to try to overcome the difficulty. The banks in that part of the zone are fully supported by the central bank and receive cash from the national system to operate day to day. Tax revenues are available to send to the badly affected region and to support banks in difficulties.

The elite set the Euro up to suffer a series of major crises. It is an orphan currency without the backing of the taxpayers in the richer parts of the zone. It is awaiting full economic and political union, when it too will have the support of a single state with a single government and taxable capacity capable of backing it properly. The need to compromise with ailing national democracies over how much power the Union wields has compromised the security and the economic success of the venture.-The Euro is subject to two main types of shock or crisis.

Little progress on state debt

If an individual member state of the Union disobeys the rules limiting the stock of debt that country is allowed, the state seeks to free ride on the back of the Union's average lower interest rates for the cost of its more excessive debt.

The Euro area has made little progress in curbing the high levels of state debt which characterised most of the members at foundation. Several countries remain at twice the permitted levels, and many are 50% or more above the permitted threshold. This is not in itself destabilising until the Union decides that a particular country needs to reduce its debt to get somewhere nearer the rules.

The Union's policy on tax and spend can be in direct conflict with the member state's policy. This is aggravated if the member state wants to continue increasing its debt by running a relatively high budget deficit. Then the rows between the Union and the country concerned become more intense as the Union seeks to define what measures the state will take to cut or eliminate the deficit in any given year.

These issues give rise to member state borrowing crises, often played out through the markets forcing up the cost of additional borrowing for the non-compliant country.

The banking system of an individual member state is also a cause of Euro crises. Individual countries remain responsible for ensuring their commercial banks are properly financed and solvent.

In recent years the European Central Bank has taken on more of the functions of a central bank regulator of commercial banks throughout the zone. The ECB lays down requirements for cash, capital and conduct, alongside banking legislation from the EU. The individual country however remains responsible for ensuring a private or public sector solution for any bank short of capital to trade, subject to EU controls on state aids.

The Germans and other surplus countries have no wish to act as guarantor of capital adequacy throughout the banks of the zone, and the EU accepts no automatic responsibility to put up the money either. If a banking system or a large individual bank is subject to runs on its deposits owing to lack of confidence in the capital and cash reserves, the member state has to take the lead in finding a solution.

There have been Euro crises from 2009 onwards. The banking crash and great recession of 2008-9 revealed the tensions within the Euro system.

A worse predicament

The EU in the early days of the US and UK crash reassured people this was a crisis of Anglo-Saxon capitalism which their different model escaped. They were soon to find themselves in a worse predicament than the US and UK, locked into the problems of their Euro rules and bound by the reluctance of the core of the zone to offer financial support to either near bankrupt governments or near bankrupt commercial banks elsewhere in the area.

Both the US and the UK recapitalised their banks quickly, and both were able to continue borrowing for state purposes at competitive rates on markets untroubled by their levels of overall borrowing. In contrast the Eurozone suffered a succession of problems affecting Ireland, Portugal, Spain, Italy, and above all Greece and Cyprus.

In each case problems were made worse by the interaction of state debt levels with the weakness of banking systems, and complicated by the impact the rigid Euro scheme had on economic performance in each country.

The overinflated economies of Spain and Ireland plunged into much deeper recession with much higher unemployment and large budget deficits as the banking crash proceeded. Both found it difficult to afford borrowing on the markets, as the cost of state debt was driven up by the absence of help from the stronger parts of the zone and from the EU wanting these countries to rein in their debt through dramatic austerity policies.

Markets worried that a Eurozone country placed under the control of EU policy makers could plunge deeper into recession making the deficits worse. This in turn could lead to demands for yet more austere austerity.

In the cases of Spain and Ireland austerity was administered but in the end market confidence was restored to enable these two to end their programmes of support from the EU and move back to being self-financing. Both countries sought and obtained special loans to get through. In Spain's case all the money was used to recapitalise weak banks.

Because the 2008-9 crisis was so tough on several Euro countries the zone did set up a fund called the European Stability Mechanism to lend money to states in distress against tough programmes of tax rises and spending cuts.

The role of the IMF

EU lending was often advanced in conjunction with the IMF as the EU sought some external validation of its very unpopular terms for its loans. Greece, Ireland, Portugal, Romania, Spain. Latvia and Hungary all needed assistance after 2010 and all came under express programmes for their budgets.

The IMF is one of the quintessential elite global quangos that has specialised in making loans to the emerging market countries, usually with strict terms attached over the conduct of their budget and economic policy.

This has often made the IMF very unpopular with countries needing help, with some critics arguing that the IMF's remedies depress demand and make recovery and growth more difficult. Others point to successful cases where IMF austerity programmes have cut inflation drastically, restored market confidence and allowed recovery.

The advent of the IMF as the saviour of the Euro came about when Christine Lagarde from the French government became the its head and decided to help the EU with IMF money and moral backing.

The Euro area and adjacent countries soon became the dominant user of IMF funds, which came as a surprise to all those who saw the IMF as mainly there to help poorer countries. The IMF never once suggested reforms to the Euro system or argued that maybe the richer parts of the Eurozone should provide the extra money the poorer parts clearly needed.

The IMF does not, for example, offer money to a region of the UK or a state within the US union when that part of a single currency zone needs more cash. The IMF rightly leaves that to the state concerned to sort out its own internal arrangements.

Yet in the case of the Eurozone the IMF was prepared to look through the Union to the individual sometimes quite small member states.

It shows the club-like nature of the global elite. As they move from grand job in an EU state to a big job in a global quango they carry with them the agenda of the elite they have just left, and come to each other's aid.

The IMF that regularly tears into the economic and political stances of governments of countries like Brazil or Argentina would not dream of being critical of the direction of the Euro project, however much economic damage it might do.

Greece's problems

In the Greek case the crisis was deeper and much more prolonged than in Ireland or Spain. What began as a state financing crisis soon became a banking crisis as well.

Greece was forced into deep spending cuts and tax rises as the crash of 2008-9 did economic damage and left the Greeks with a large state deficit. Far from making things better, the austerity policies led to further steep falls in employment, output and incomes.

Greece went through a succession of struggles with the EU over the size of financial assistance and the terms of the loans. She reneged on state debts held by the private sector to try to cut the burden of historic debt, which damaged the banking system elsewhere in the zone where banks held substantial quantities of Greek debt.

Youth unemployment soared to more than 60% and general unemployment was close to 30%. Austerity programmes included large cuts in public sector pay, substantial public sector redundancies and cuts in pensions. Greek national income fell by more than a third.

Some have argued that practically all the money advanced under EU loans to troubled countries has gone in help to commercial banks throughout the zone who were left holding state debt from troubled countries.

These bad economic outturns caused continuous political disruption. Both the traditional centre left and centre right Greek parties, Pasok and New Democracy, were voted into office to resolve the economic meltdown and failed.

In desperation the public then voted in a new party of the left, Syriza, with a majority to reverse the austerity budgets that were doing so much harm. Syriza embarked on such a course, only to encounter strong resistance from the EU. The EU withheld financial support to force compliance, and threatened the Greeks with exit from the Euro altogether if they refused to pay by the rules. To ratchet up the pressure further the EU used its ultimate weapon against a non-compliant Euro state. The ECB withheld cash needed by the Greek banking system.

This last action brought Greece into line quickly. Banks were shut altogether for 20 days. People were only allowed to withdraw €60 a day from cash machines.

Businesses needed central bank authority to move money out of their accounts to pay bills over a small threshold. A sophisticated modern economy cannot function without a full banking system to allow and make payments. The government and Greek people eventually decided they wanted to stay in the Euro and needed access to Euro cash, so they went along with another tough programme of spending cuts and tax rises.

Cyprus too saw action at the hands of the European Central Bank. The crisis was mainly driven in Cyprus by the overextension of a large banking sector relative to the size of the host economy.

The ECB withdrew financial support from banks it believed to be overextended, whilst the EU forced the Cyprus authorities to require large depositors in some Cypriot banks to lose a share of the Euros deposited in the banks as part of the cost of dealing with the banks' financial problems.

It turned out that a Euro deposited in Cyprus was not worth the same as a Euro deposited in Germany. One large bank was shut down altogether. Like Greeks, Cypriots discovered that in the Eurozone you could be locked out from your bank and prevented from spending or drawing out your own money, as ordinary businesses and individual customers found their cash was detained and even taken from you by the bigger pressures. In a normal single country currency zone, the central bank does not stop sending cash needed by commercial banks in deficit towns or regions.

The stresses in the zone remain great. Underlying the two big generators of crises, overspending governments and broken banks, lies the payments imbalances between the member states.

There is no longer a balance of payments in the normal sense that you have between two separate countries.

We do not talk about a UK region running a balance of payments deficit with London, if it does. Flows of government money, tax revenue, and commercial banking transactions ensure any deficit is financed and any surplus is reused within the sterling zone.

What the UK accepts

The UK government accepts financial obligations to every part of the UK and sends tax revenue as needed to pay bills. The Bank of England and the clearing banks meet demands for cash anywhere in the currency zone without worrying whether the town or region is in surplus or deficit.

The Eurozone has not been prepared to do this. The EU refuses to recycle the large sums recycled in, say the UK, by the tax and benefits and local government finance system. The ECB in some cases refuses cash to banks within its zone, even though it regulates them as solvent institutions.

In practice the EU and the ECB have had to give some ground from the Germanic discipline that lay behind the ECB's establishment.

Many countries, including Germany, maintain substantially higher state debt levels than are laid down in the rules. The zone is much more hawkish about budget deficits, where Germany strictly adheres to the common rules.

The reason the system has not been torn apart by the pressures in the way the ERM was is simple. The European Central Bank now sends the money around the zone from rich to poor in place of a system of regional subsidies and regional financial support. The method is through a scheme known as Target 2 balances.

Germany, the main country in surplus, deposits her surplus Euros in the ECB from selling so many exports. She accepts the ECB covenant on the money and is paid no interest on it. Italy, Spain, Portugal and Greece, the main deficit countries that need to borrow to pay for their imports and their excess public spending, borrow under the same scheme at zero interest. There is no specified repayment date.

This system began as a short-term facility to smooth out surpluses and deficits between the different commercial banks of the zone. It has become by proxy a way of financing the deficit countries through their banking systems at no cost as if it were a grant.

It has provided much needed stability in an inherently unstable system. As long as Germany does not want her money back, and as long as it stays at zero interest, it allows the single currency to rub along as if it had a single sovereign government and taxpayer base. Germany has lent €930bn so far, and Italy as the biggest user has borrowed €500bn.

In the recent strife between the Italian radical coalition government and the EU both sides avoided mentioning this fundamental feature of their relationship.

What the EU and Italy didn't do

If the EU had threatened to withhold money to Italian banks in the way it did to Greece and Cyprus it would have won, but at a massive price in terms of market and economic damage. If Italy had refused to cut its spending at all and demanded that they implement in their budget what they promised their electors to win the election they may have forced the EU into considering extreme action through the bank. It is good they have not done so, so the Euro lives another life.

Today the Euro remains an orphan currency. It is still not properly backed by all the taxpayers of the zone and by a reliable government that enforces the same system everywhere in the zone.

The Euro's life will continue to be exciting, with possible periodic crises if and when different member states are thought to have gone too far in breaking the rules.

The elite have introduced a currency without explaining the full exchange of power from national to EU level it requires. This selective explanation means the currency they have fostered is subject to scares and alarms no normal single currency faces. It also means the inherent tensions and contradictions can only be finally resolved by full political union.

When German tax revenue is EU tax revenue, then Greece and Italy can be properly financed and be genuinely part of the same currency and nation. When a deficit in a bank in Greece is automatically covered from the surpluses of banks elsewhere, then the system will work smoothly. The elite have inadvertently encouraged challenger parties and radical politics, as a reaction to the tough austerity trying to live within the Eurozone forces on more than half its member states.

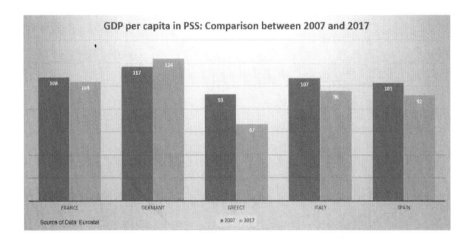

GDP per capita in PSS: Comparison between 2007 and 2017

Source of Data: Eurostat ▪ 2007 ▪ 2017

Chapter 3

Why does the elite like high levels of migration?

Across the West there are now populists on the march against immigration. When this protest becomes unpleasant it can cross the legal line rightly laid down against racism and incitement to hatred

Migration has been one of the biggest flare points between the global elite and the populist movements.

To the elite migration is a good thing. They welcome willing labour coming into countries that are successful at creating more jobs. They like the erosion of national loyalties and outlooks, as more people take a wider or global perspective. They as citizens of nowhere want more to join them in their perceived global village. They wish to loosen the ties of place and culture, to challenge national and local perceptions and attitudes.

To the settled communities that accept the arrival of many new people this can look altogether different. Some fear the erosion of old truths and certainties and changes to traditional lifestyles. Some think the advent of much more labour means lower wages and more difficulty finding a job.

Some are afraid of people with different cultures and values, and look for the worst by highlighting any criminal conduct by a minority of the new arrivals. Some doubt the elite idea that a country will be richer if it offers open house to newcomers, citing the costs of welfare, housing and subsidising lower wages.

The background to the rows over migration are fourfold.

- The first are the intense religious and civil wars waging especially in the Middle East. This has created large numbers of displaced persons, and many more who decide it would be better to be an economic migrant than to hang around waiting for disaster where they were born.

- The second is the rapid change brought about by the digital economy, creating a global market for most goods and many services. This allows people to compete from a low income country at lower wages, or to move to a richer country to compete directly in their labour market.
- The third is the growing volume of exchanges particularly in the field of education where many more want to study abroad and learn English in particular.
- The fourth is the role of multinational companies in insisting on a diverse or multi country workforce in any given territory.

Much damage has been done by the great religious wars and factional and tribal struggles in the Middle East.

In Syria alone it is estimated 5.6m Syrians were displaced by the war there and live outside the country, whilst another 6.2m displaced Syrians are sheltering somewhere else in their own country.

There were around one million Libyan refugees from the conflict in that country. Yemen, Iran, Afghanistan and many other Middle Eastern states are generating displaced people or economic migrants owing to the uncertainties, wars and purges underway.

Taken globally the UN estimated in 2017 there were 65.5m displaced people, of whom 24.5m were refugees seeking shelter in a new host country.

Many of these people wanted to come to the USA, the UK or the EU to find greater political stability, a stronger rule of law, and more relatively well paid job opportunities.

The harrowing scenes of war have appeared on our tv screens showing people maimed and killed by barrel bombs or intense fires or shelling in urban landscapes. These have plucked heartstrings in the West and provided a reason why so many are taking to the roads and seas to get out of the danger zones. Others not under such threat in their African or Middle Eastern states also join the refugees from violence in travelling to seek a better life.

These troubling scenes have also led to some bitter politics.

Populist anti migrant parties have sprung up casting doubt on the authenticity of some of the films of refuges. They have queried how many are genuinely fleeing terror, and how many are economic migrants from safer places using the civil war of Syria or the conflict in the Yemen as cover for their movement.

The elite point to the suffering and in the name of humanity take decisions to help. Some of the populists ask is there some limit to numbers? How can the west cope? Are these all true cases? Why are so many of the new arrivals young men? Where are the families and the older people?

What digital does

The power of the digital revolution sweeps much before it.

It makes it so much easier to set up a business anywhere in the world and advertise on the internet. It allows people in low income high unemployment countries to see the openings and opportunities in richer countries many hundreds or thousands of miles away. It leads more to calculate that travelling to these lands of milk and honey might be worth the effort. It propels more economic migrants from Africa and the Middle East and from parts of Asia to head towards Europe and the USA.

The business models of UK and US universities used to major on recruiting and teaching young people from their own societies. In more recent decades universities on both sides of the Atlantic have wanted to expand their activities and tap new sources of fee income and endowment wealth.

This has led them to expand more through offers to the many from outside their countries to come to learn and to live in the USA or UK.

To attract people they often indicate a willingness to help the student on graduation get a first job in the UK or US as part of the package. Whilst the universities cannot sell the students the guarantee of citizenship, they can hint that coming as a student and taking advantage of the ability to undertake some work on graduating gets the person closer to being able to apply for citizenship.

Rules over entitlement to better paid jobs and for prolonged stays for well qualified people also strengthen the case for someone to come legally as a student and see what avenues open up.

Most countries like attracting inward investment from large multinational companies. In a world of global brands where people are likely to buy Mercedes cars or Coca Cola drinks or use Google services there is a premium on attracting investment and employment by these large companies that service the individual country in the context of its wider global brand management.

These companies often want to inject management and skilled personnel into a new territory when they establish there, requiring work permits and migration of talent. They also often want the teams and management cadres to be filled with a wide range of people from different religious, cultural and country backgrounds, as they seek to understand the differences between national markets.

They look to find a common way through for product and services, but in so doing wish to incorporate features – and exclude features – that meet the widest possible degree of acceptance. This requires a global workforce of people whose main loyalties are to their company and the wider world, who can draw on their knowledge of their old national culture and the national culture of other places where they have worked for the corporation. These executives are indeed often citizens of nowhere, committed to a global perspective.

This background has produced some big increases in migrant numbers in recent years. Some 44m people living in the USA or 13% of the population are people not born in the country.

It is true the USA has a long history of substantial inward migration from the times of the early English settlers through successive waves of largely European migration in the nineteenth century.

There was also the long period of slave trade migration which casts a shadow.

More recently the migration has been primarily from Hispanic and Latino locations, followed by substantial Asian migration. In 2016 an additional 1.5m arrived in the USA, with the states of California, New York, Florida, Texas and New Jersey taking the largest numbers. For the first time in the USA there are now communities where Spanish, not English is the principal language.

UK migration

In the UK net migration has been running at 250,000 or more for a decade, compared to the 50,000 additional people a year more common in the last century. The net figure conceals the gross inward migration figure of more than 600,000 or almost 1% of the population a year, by taking off the substantial number of emigrants.

It means the pace of change in the population is much faster than the net figure suggests.

Each new migrant needs housing and finding a job. The high pace of change lay behind some of the build-up in support for UKIP as much of the extra migration came from Eastern Europe under EU rules following the admission to membership of those additional countries. It was also part of the unofficial campaign to leave the EU carried on by Leave EU, but was not encouraged by the official Leave campaign.

Germany has recently experienced tough political reactions to a sharp acceleration in the rate of migration in the mid 2010s.

By 2015 migration into Germany reached the highly visible one million mark which upset many supporters of Mrs Merkel and fuelled support for the AFD, which became more of an anti-migrant party and less of an anti-Euro organisation as a result.

The Christian Democrats lost substantial support as voters looked for a way of expressing their dislike of such a large flow of people into their country. There were various news stories where anti migrant people sought to highlight crimes committed by a few of the new arrivals, and sought to make cultural differences an issue.

The upset of inward migration

So what is it about high levels of inward migration that causes so much upset?

Why should this fuel political change and provide additional votes to radical alternative parties? There is both an economic case and a cultural case to consider.

The people most likely to object to high levels of migration are those in jobs prone to be subject to competition from incoming labour, or to be unemployed who resent foreigners coming and taking jobs they might need for themselves.

The people most likely to favour high levels of inward migration are business leaders who seek easier recruitment, or rich people who want flexible employees to help them in their daily lives at cheaper rates of pay.

The executive couple may want an au pair or cleaner or nanny or general assistant. Quite often people from abroad from low income countries are willing to work long and flexible hours and accept pay packages that may not be attractive to local individuals.

For companies there is a temptation for well trained and well educated new arrivals to undertake less skilled work than they could manage in order to get established and earn a living. They often show high levels of commitment and can go on to accept more responsibility.

There is also a nasty illegal market in people trafficking where economic migrants buy illegal access to a country. They agree to undertake work often provided by a criminal gang, and to live in poor accommodation provided by the racketeers. The modern slave trade is a blot on western societies. Governments want to eradicate it, but relatively open borders and the large scale of official migration makes enforcement more difficult.

Policy dilemmas

This produces a policy dilemma for governments and a recruitment dilemma for companies.

On the one hand governments want to expand their economies easily and might welcome people in with good qualifications willing to be flexible. On the other hand governments should have a prior obligation to established voters and residents who may need more help and training to take the various jobs on offer.

It is not good politics to rely on importing new labour if a pool of potential labour is left behind and out of work, or stuck in low paid low skilled roles.

It also produces a problem for companies. They may well usually incline to what they see as the easier option of hiring more people from overseas but they need to understand their role in the local community where they are based. Modern business has to appreciate the importance of being a good neighbour as a business, and to develop the social role of business and employment in a community.

Good governments work with business to try to secure decent training and ensure opportunity for advancement within larger companies. They also keep a balance between the ability to invite new labour in from outside, with the wish to give plenty of opportunity to people already settled in the country and in need of work or wanting better paid and more highly skilled work.

At the bottom end of the pay scales may well be work that could be best done by machine power and artificial intelligence. Productivity policy needs to help send the right signals to business about the need for investment in labour saving technology to replace poor and low paid jobs. This will also require sensible controls over work permits and other entry devices.

There have been various studies to demonstrate that there is some downwards pressure on wages where large scale migration is permitted or encouraged.

By definition if you increase supply then the price is likely to fall. There has not been the same attention to the issue of productivity, where it might go either way. The presence of more people to do low paid jobs may be keeping down the rate of productivity enhancing investment, whilst the presence of more people enthusiastic to work well may help.

Economic benefits?

The argument over the economic benefit has been intense but not well informed.

Official surveys purporting to suggest that in the UK new migrants add value has concentrated on looking at the narrow issue of business added value compared to in work benefits and tax paid. These usually conclude that there is a net gain per migrant employed. They do not look at the longer term costs where the migrant settles and comes with their family to qualify for a much wider range of benefits and public services.

More importantly it does not look at the first year set up costs, which largely fall on other taxpayers.

Many migrants need social housing in a country short of such provision. Each additional social housing unit costs, say, £100,000 to provide, with a much higher cost in London and the south east where many migrants find jobs and chose to live.

They need extra provision for GP surgeries and hospital capacity, and require school places if they have children once here or arrive with children.

There is then the need to provide additional train and road capacity to cope with substantial increases in passengers and vehicle miles travelled. The EU itself put an indicative €250,000 as the set up cost for a new migrant arriving in the EU to remind countries of the extent of the financial commitment.

It is the pressure on homes and other public facilities that causes some of the resentment amongst those who dislike large scale migration.

If you or one of your family members is on a council or housing association waiting list for a suitable residence you may well feel unhappy if you see new arrivals gaining greater priority for the homes that do become available.

If a popular school fills up its places quickly and forces parents to accept a less popular or less successful alternative, that too can cause resentment at the parents and pupils who were successful.

There is general worry about the adequacy of NHS GP provision, where fears can be increased if there is a rapid rate of population growth and additional pressure of numbers on local facilities. All of this can be taken care of by good government planning, and putting more investment in in good time for the expansion of population. Unfortunately this does not always happen.

It still leaves open the issue of the alleged economic benefits of migration.

From the state and taxpayer point of view it is difficult to see how the state makes a profit on large volumes of low paid migration. Much of the low pay is now tax free, and attracts in-work benefit top ups.

The need to provide housing, welfare, healthcare, transport and education with some high initial capital costs means the state and taxpayer has an up-front cost to pay for some of low-paid employees that arrive. This does not mean it is wrong, but it has led to distrust of those who advocate more migration for claiming that the state makes an in year profit every year on each person invited in to the UK.

The figures for higher remunerated migrants are more economically favourable for the host country.

They pay more tax from day one, and may come with some capital of their own. They may provide their own housing and raise their own loan to buy a property.

There are still the longer term issues to consider, and of course the favourable economic outcome relies on their continued good health and employment. These narrow economic arguments, however, overlay more potentially emotional issues.

The issue of change

Many people are wary of change. They have invested their own time and trouble in the mores and culture of their local community. The education of the more elderly was based on a settled view of the world that was rather different to the modern more global digitalised world.

Underneath the arguments over housing shortages and financial contributions to the state are questions of what kind of community do people live in, and how much change of personnel can there be before there is a marked shift in the nature of that community?

The populists think there has to be some limit on how many people to invite in to any particular village or town so there can be continuity of character and behaviour. Modernisers welcome a faster pace of change and look forward to the changes of traditions, events and cultures that will bring about .

This comes down to the big debate about whether society should just be very tolerant and welcome greater diversity of culture, language, religion, diet and mores, or whether there needs to be more integration, with the new arrivals adopting more of the language, culture and styles of the community they join.

In practice in the UK today we aim for a bit of both. People are encouraged to learn and use English to improve their life chances and help them in employment. They are asked to pass a citizens' test with basic knowledge of the country they are joining. They are free to practise the religion of their choice, to belong to groups and families as they see fit and to choose their own diet and private lifestyle which may be very different from the typical one of the settled community they have joined. The compromise is pushed from both sides. The advocates of more tolerance seek to reduce the pressures for integration, whilst others want to eliminate more of the differences.

To some extent this contrast is a generational matter.

The first generation arriving from a foreign country may have difficulty in learning the language and accepting the different customs and behaviours.

The children are born and brought up here and educated usually in mainstream UK schools, so they assimilate naturally more of the average or settled culture of the community.

Lord Tebbitt put it very bluntly when he claimed that someone was integrated or properly part of the UK community when they supported England at cricket whoever the country might be playing at the time. That was his rough measure of how someone saw their identity. Others thought this was intolerant.

What is undeniably true is the issue of migration is one of the issues that most sparks fierce and emotional responses from both sides in the elite versus the public debate.

The elite see accepting large numbers of migrants as a test of a civilised country. They argue that it is economically good for the host country, but there is underneath a strong moral argument that a rich society has a duty to open its doors wide to the poor of the world and to help as many as possible to improve their living standards by coming and working in an advanced economy.

They regard critics of this position as racist or unacceptably hostile to certain religious groups. They pass laws to try to enforce a decent tolerance ,and require people to behave to high standards in word and deed to make a friendly multi-cultural society possible.

The Christian religion has through its established churches been a voice for more tolerance of others and more migrants to be sheltered in the West. At the same time Christian institutions have had to live with a growing intolerance and even violent hostility to Christians in some parts of the world.

The fear of migration led President Trump to campaign to extend the border wall with Mexico that President Clinton started.

He responded to fears of cheap labour from the south driving down wages with a promise of a physical barrier. This horrified the elites and the Democrats, who forgot Mr Clinton's role in this.

The EU too condemned the Trump idea, only for member states of the Union to put in many more miles of border fence and walls as they struggled to cut the surge of migration into Europe around 2015.

The EU spoke of the need to be generous and to be tolerant, but in the end acted to stifle the high levels of inward migration understanding the substantial political hostility to it.

At the fringes of the populist uprisings there is an anti-foreigner impetus, fuelled by dislike of cultural and religious differences. The way this is introduced into the debate is usually via criticism of foreign criminals, playing on fears of terrorism and violent crime in the wider community.

What begins as a move to stop criminals or potential terrorists coming into the country can elide with the racist minority who wish to imply that certain backgrounds produce a much higher tendency to terrorist or violent behaviour than others.

The West has put in place laws against hate crimes to try to contain this type of unacceptable pressure. Governments have to deal with hard cases where known terrorists have gained access to a new country despite their past criminal records or despite the Intelligence services knowing and fearing things about them. In Germany the issue of crime committed by recently arrived migrants became a big concern at the height of the migrations.

Some of the populists see this migration as wrong. They think it is self-serving by the elites who want to import cheap labour to keep the pay of the working class down, and to employ cheap personal assistants to improve their gilded lifestyles.

They disagree with the figures put out to suggest we are all better off thanks to the flow of low paid migrants, and see in their difficulty to find a social housing home or get a pay rise evidence that migration is doing them harm.

All across the EU and the USA there are now populists on the march. They are saying "We don't believe you" when the elites tell them that migration is good for them and good for their living standards. When this protest becomes unpleasant it can cross the legal line rightly laid down against racism and incitement to hatred.

Chapter 4

The revolt of the motorist

Many voters see one rule for the rich and one for the rest in global warming policies – another case of a big disconnect between those who govern and the populists who have to live with their ideas and actions

The elite have their own religion. They are genuinely concerned that man-made global warming is the biggest threat to humankind.

They never hold an international meeting or economic conference these days without repeating the message about climate change.

We are told that unless people mend their ways promptly and use much less fossil fuel, there will be a dangerous sea rise, many more cyclones and tsunamis, and all manner of economic damage as the climate gets nastier. The polar ice caps will melt.

The message infuses every quango. The mainstream broadcasters pour out their warnings and feast on interviews with the elite spokesmen and women most exercised by this looming tragedy. Most global governments tailor their policies on transport, energy and much else to the imperative need to cut carbon dioxide emissions.

They have latched on to the laws of thermodynamics and the theory of radiative transfer to tell us all that the science of climate change is settled. They close down debate on it by stating that anyone who dares to disagree with either their belief that this is a serious threat, or with their proposed remedies, is a climate change denier.

These echoes of the language used to describe those who against all the evidence deny the holocaust is particularly telling. They argue that a further warming will melt the ice sheets, raise sea levels so high that great coastal cities will be swamped, and fear the advent of many more extreme weather events that will destroy crops and lead to suffering and deaths. These would indeed be dreadful consequences and need to be seriously considered.

A significant part of the public in countries like the USA and UK are not persuaded. They are sceptical of some of the more extreme claims, and put off by the unwillingness of the elite to engage in debate or further research into what is actually happening.

Most of the climate change sceptics of course accept the scientific underpinnings of the argument.

They accept that carbon dioxide, nitrous oxide, water vapour and methane are greenhouse gases. They accept that the earth warms up from sunlight, and stays warm if there is sufficient greenhouse gas in the lower atmosphere to prevent too much heat dissipation through radiation back to space. They accept that with many more people living on the planet burning fuels and finding other ways to generate carbon dioxide, there will be more human produced carbon dioxide around. There are few deniers of all this.

What the so-called deniers want to examine more carefully is what else influences climate.

They ask the elite to explain why there were periods of global warming punctuated by ice ages long before man was on the planet, and during the pre-industrial period of human life.

Could the causes of these cycles still be at work moulding current climate trends?

- What role does the sun play, with variable activity levels and variable intensity of output over time?
- What is the role of water vapour, which is both a greenhouse gas tending to warm us up, and in the form of clouds an obvious force to keep the surface temperature down by screening out direct sunlight?
- How do the complex climate change models needed model long-term cloud intensity and coverage?
- What exactly is the rate of ice melt and why does it appear to be different at the two poles?
- Why is there no complete explanation of pre-industrial ice ages and warming periods?
- How good have the human-based CO2 models been at predicting past climate changes?

- What has been the actual rate of temperature rise, as some observed data suggest interruptions in temperature rises in recent decades when manmade CO2 has been most intense?

Sensible climate change sceptics do not deny the theoretical underpinnings of the science but want to refine what is said and improve on the predictions.

There have been premature predictions about temperature and consequences so far. Sceptics also remember that 50 years ago some scientists were predicting a new cold era. Some other sceptics do fully accept the models and the predictions, but think adaptation and managing effects is a better response than trying to prevent all the Carbon dioxide.

The elite claim they have covered all or most of these issues in their complex models, but have not been able to persuade some of the public who do not think they have explained it properly.

The questioners are treated as people incapable of understanding the "settled science".

If the deniers are scientists they are often left out of access to funding for more research or have their research credentials, right to publish and entitlement to tenured jobs limited by their espousal of an unpopular view within their profession.

Some thought the whole point of scientific method was to put up a hypothesis or theory, to get others to try and shoot it down or improve it by challenging it. In the case of global warming we are assured the theory is already perfect and anyone who doubts it is simply wrong.

Reinforcing the message

The elite reinforce their message that the climate is warming, that warming is harmful, and that the cause is man-made carbon dioxide. They sometimes accept that methane too is a partial cause, incriminating dairy and meat eaters through the generation of methane by cows and beef cattle.

They wish to attack the use of fossil fuels as the main cause within this explanation, and get on to the policy debate about how to do it.

As their principal remedy is effectively to put the price of fossil fuel derived energy up, it can get them into conflict with many voters, especially all those on considerably lower incomes than the elite who have difficulty in paying the higher energy bills which result.

Policy has centred around increasing taxes on energy use and energy generation by the wrong means.

Governments impose high taxes on motor fuels, taxes on domestic fuels, carbon taxes on electricity generation and industrial processes, sales taxes on energy, bidding premia and licence charges on companies extracting oil, gas and coal, and carbon pricing with quotas that require expenditure to acquire the right to burn.

There are also an increasing number of physical controls or bans, preventing exploitation of some resources, and removal or denial of permits for certain types of engine and vehicle.

The case for these tough actions is set out by Friends of the Earth, one of the pressure groups that encourage this approach to government.

As it states on its website "Climate change is devastating people's lives all over the world. With droughts, storms, floods, crop damage and sea level rise, millions are fleeing their homes and it's the poorest who are hardest hit".

"The evils of fossil fuel"

Governments and quangos see themselves locked in a race against time and against the evils of the fossil fuel exploiting industry and the industries and homes that live off these suppliers of heat and power. They both try to stop the conduct that they think is so damaging by high taxes and regulation, and try to proffer alternative options in each case through subsidy and exhortation.

In some areas there is a happy consensus of view between the elite and the governed. Few deny it is a good approach to insulate buildings more so there is less need to burn fuels to keep warm or to cool the place down in summer.

Most welcome research and development to produce more fuel-efficient generations of vehicles and machines. These are benign commonsense policies that save people money by cutting their use of fuel.

There is also general agreement on the priority to get down emissions which make air dirty and unpleasant to breathe.

The language of green campaigners is often aimed against dirty pollution. To the campaigner this may include CO2. To many members of the public this invisible gas that is not directly harmful if breathed in as part of the air we breathe is not in the same category as smoke or particulates which are both dirty and dangerous.

Where many populist voters and the elite start to diverge is over individual solutions to the problem of how we reduce CO2.

The main target they have in mind is the petrol and diesel car. Private vehicle traffic is accorded a special place in the demonology of the global warming theorists, blamed more than its proportion of CO2 generated. There is little attention to the CO2 output of trains and less to buses than to cars.

All transport seems to attract more anger than domestic heating boilers, though these are a substantial part of the problem.

It is the concentration on cars that causes much of the tension between the governments and the dissenters on this issue.

Members of the public see the attacks on use of a private car as an attack upon their freedom of movement which they value highly. The car is often the way to get to work, the means to take children to school, and the source of much pleasure taking the family to events, leisure activities, friends and family gatherings. People see their vehicle as an important part of their social lives, not as the creator of a global weather crisis. The Gilet Jaune protests in France began by demanding cheaper vehicle fuel.

The elites have adopted various policies to discourage car use.

In the UK the authorities have been particularly keen to cut down the amount of usable road space for private cars in busy areas as the number of vehicles has risen.

Pedestrianisation, bus and cycle lanes, road closures, congestion charges, extra delays at junctions have all been deployed to drive more people out of their cars. High levels of Vehicle Excise Duty and fuel tax are designed to deter ownership and use of a car.

There is considerable use of train options at morning and evening peaks given the very congested state of the roads, but at other times of day the superior flexibility of the car often prevails.

People like the way their car is at home ready to go anytime they wish, with access to most places they want to visit. In contrast off peak trains may be few and far between, and only go to stations which might be some way from home and from the planned destination, requiring a car or taxi ride as well.

Encouraging electric cars

Aware of the difficult task of arguing and taxing people out of their own vehicles, governments have also decided to try to get people to buy electric cars instead of petrol or diesel vehicles.

So far there has been no great rush to take up electric cars. It is a top-down change, not one driven by customer enthusiasm for the advantages of the new product.

Many buyers are put off by the high prices that still prevail for the electric car. Some are worried about the short range of many of them, and by the long time it takes to recharge the batteries. There is still a shortage of official recharging points, though of course anywhere with an electricity supply can become a charging point with the right connectors.

Governments are seeking to make electric cars more attractive by subsidising the original purchase, by exempting them from taxes that apply to petrol and diesel vehicles, and by pointing out the electric car avoids the special taxes on fossil fuel.

The public is a bit nervous about some of these offers. Governments claim to impose taxes on vehicles and fuel for environmental reasons, but it is also obvious they need the cash and see motorists as a relatively easy target.

If electric cars take off as governments plan, the public assumes new taxes will be introduced on them to deal with the loss of revenue otherwise experienced.

Distrust of governments by motorists is particularly high, as they feel they have been mugged and cheated all too often whilst the same government seeks to make their lives more difficult. Why would a change of technology alter that approach?

Governments have more mixed views on air travel. True green campaigners see flying as one of the worst manifestations of the fossil fuel economy. The elites tend to see it differently, as they like meeting each other in international gatherings and enjoy flying at other people's expense to negotiate, trade and meet with like-minded people in a wide range of other countries.

Clearly stopping so much foreign travel for holidays would save a lot of fuel burn, but it would also be a very unpopular attack upon people's enjoyment.

Governments have largely confined themselves to taxes on fuel and some taxes on transit or ticket purchase, as part of their preferred policy of making it more difficult for lower income people to burn fossil fuels. This has not tended to work for air travel, given the strong competitive forces bringing into being a large number of economy airlines offering great deals for travellers. Discount airlines have offset much of the extra tax burden by cutting ticket prices.

Railways in favour

Railways seem to be the favourite means of travel for the anti-global warming set.

In the UK the rail budget catering for 8% of our journeys is far larger than the roads budget catering for 90%.

Plenty of energy and propaganda is pumped out to get more people to travel by train. This is not always the way to cut carbon dioxide emissions as advertised.

Many trains out of peaks run with very few passengers. UK trains are particularly heavy and some require large amounts of diesel fuel to make the journey.

The passenger may well need a bus, car or taxi either end to complete the route, adding to the emissions. Train manufacture requires substantial carbon dioxide generating processes. Even electric trains draw current from the grid which in turn relies on fossil fuel sources for much of the output.

To some populists ever ready for ideas of a conspiracy, it seems the elite favour trains for others as a means of control.

The car offers you much freedom over timing, route and destination. The train requires you to be at a station at a specified time, and only allows you to go one route at a stated pace. Your journey is known to the authorities through the ticketing system. Members of the elite themselves often prefer a chauffeured car service or internal flights, liking door to door or faster long distance travel. The hypocrisy of this approach adds to the gap between governed and government.

The anti-global warming campaign is also trying to reform the use of fossil fuels in every home.

In the UK there has been debate about the idea of banning wood-burning stoves as they are seen as being anti-environmental. This is particularly interesting given the switch of some coal-fired power stations to burning wood, renamed as biomass. It is not a big issue in the scheme of things as relatively few people today burn wood in a domestic grate or specialised burner.

Domestic fuel is taxed though it is a basic necessity, and high bills are seen as a means to get people to insulate more and burn less. Governments would like people to replace their boilers with more fuel efficient models. They do initiate some subsidised work to raise thermal insulation standards and to improve control systems on heating installations.

The public see much of this as another attempt to tax them too heavily. If you are on a low income and struggling to pay your heating bills, you do not have the ready cash available to install a more efficient boiler or to insulate your home to higher standards. Once again it seemed the elite were out to attack the poorest working members of society, those who paid the bills but do not get much state aid.

The governments also tackle how we generate our power. Combined cycle gas power stations used to be the most efficient and cheapest ways to create electricity. The substitution of gas for coal drove up thermal efficiency considerably and drove down the amount of unpleasant emissions coming from the power station chimneys.

For a period the UK had a green policy it liked. The dash for gas in the 1980s and 1990s cut down particulates in the air, lowered electricity prices, and created more jobs in the offshore gas industry around our coast. It also cut carbon dioxide output. The advent of the anti-global warming policies led to the early closure of coal stations in their entirety, and pressure to move from gas powered to renewables.

One of the oddest decisions was to prefer wood over coal. The argument ran that the right type of wood, or biomass, was a renewable source through natural growth of trees. During their growth phase they absorb carbon dioxide, so it was fine to burn them.

Coal in contrast was laid down many millions of years ago so its base in old trees was not the same as new trees. To fuel Drax in the UK by biomass required importing large quantities of wood from across the Atlantic, imposing more fuel burning by the transport to get the wood here.

The experts quoted the carbon cycle and held to their view this was an environmentally friendly biomass project. Some of the public thought it was a grand wood burning stove that would not help much and would still have dirty emissions to clean up.

The growth of the wind turbine

In the EU the preferred renewable of choice became wind power.

Expensive wind turbines sprung up thanks to a welter of subsidies and regulations favouring it over fossil fuel generation. Renewable power supply was given priority to use and sell it when the wind blew.

This undermined the economics of the back up power from gas or some other alternative. Gas became a stand by power, which was dear to produce for limited periods, given the high proportion of capital cost in the total cost.

Meanwhile wind became profitable thanks to priority and favourable contracts. The total cost of generating went up considerably, as the cheapest form of generation, gas, was now dearer as it was a part-time solution. T

he wind power came down in price thanks to economies of scale on equipment allied to the subsidies, but overall total cost rose substantially.

If you need expensive back up power for when the wind does not blow it is going to be dearer than just running the back up as baseload.

Germany started to experience some blackouts when the wind let the system down.

The UK tells big business users that they have to be ready to stop using power if a shortage of wind coincides with high demand. The public is left wondering why the system has to be changed to be both dearer and less reliable.

Once again it is the lower paid people who suffer most, as fuel is a higher proportion of their total spend and they feel the higher prices more.

The anti-global warming advocates are well organised, influential and keen to drive on with their revolution.

They want to see transport transformed away from one person one car to a more collective model. They want to see power generated almost entirely from renewable sources. They want to redesign the home, the city and the government, and to be global in reach and aspiration.

Much of the work has been done through huge international conferences seeking to bind countries to ever stricter targets of lower CO_2 along with all the intermediate targets that implies for vehicles homes and businesses. At its best their work is very helpful, as it can assist in cutting harmful emissions and in raising fuel efficiency substantially, which is a win win for all.

In the USA Trump supporters on the whole do not agree that global warming is a real problem.

They point to indeterminate figures for temperatures and climate patterns, or assert that weather has always been variable but difficult to predict.

They do not think there is a major threat. They also think it impossible for the world to rein in its carbon dioxide even if were true. They argue that China and other developing nations are busy building more fossil fuel power stations and buying many more cars. Why should the USA rein in her demand for energy when countries with many more people are going to consume so much more?

Donald Trump spoke for the coal miners, for the oil employees and the gas companies when he decided to back more lower cost fossil fuel power for the USA. He wishes to onshore more lost manufacturing jobs, and regards a plentiful supply of good value power as crucial to this mission. It also generates more and better paid jobs in the energy industries themselves.

The battle over fracking

The battle over trying to grow the oil and gas businesses has become focussed on one particular technique often used in gas and oil extraction.

Fracking is the means by which an oil or gas producer ensures the rock structure that acts as a fuel reservoir is sufficiently porous to allow the gas or oil to flow out through the wells to the surface. This may entail injecting water to increase reservoir pressure and force the oil or gas up. It may entail putting down certain chemicals to loosen or fracture the reservoir rock.

Those keenest to keep the oil and gas underground to avoid more being burned argue that these techniques can be damaging to those on the surface, both by destabilising the rocks and by possibly polluting water.

The industry replies that there is no large seismic effect as the rocks are loosened, and certainly no big collapses as there can be with underground coal mining. They claim to take tough action to ensure no chemicals leach into water that is used for water supply, and the oil and gas reservoirs are usually at a very different level in the strata from the aquifer.

In the UK too there are sceptics about the climate changes being experienced, and doubts about the ability of climate models to predict the weather in three months' time, let alone a hundred years hence.

There is the same doubt about how much of a difference the UK can make to the huge energy use worldwide, based on the UK's much smaller and declining contribution to total world carbon dioxide output.

The arguments about fracking are more intense in the UK than in the USA, with every new onshore well bitterly contested by those who want to limit use of carbon based fuels. This causes the elite to condemn the public and urge them to greater sacrifices to get their use of fossil fuels down.

To the populists the elite appears to live in a different world where they afford the high fuel prices they impose and use chauffeured cars and planes where others are told to go by bus.

Global warming theory leads to anti car policies many voters dislike. It imposes what populists call thought control on people as their children are taught the new religion and condemned for questioning it.

Some campaign against more windmills near them. They complain of their noise, and of the harm they do to birds. Some protest against dear fuel prices. Many enjoy the exposure of hypocrisy, when social media or parts of the press capture the elite in large buildings blazing with lights.

Elite travel patterns to attend global warming conferences by limousine and fuel-hungry jets also get singled out. The elite has a new religion. Many electors see it as an attack on their living standard and way of life.

In France higher energy taxes triggered major riots and forced President Macron to back down over some of his measures. The protesters put a lot of speed cameras out of action in response to reduced speed limits to cut fuel use.

They see one rule for the rich and one for the rest. It leads many voters to say to governments when it comes to their global warming policies, we don't believe you. This is another case of a big disconnection between those who govern and the populists who have to live with their ideas and actions.

Chapter 5

The Christian Democrats and Social Democrats fall under a populist tide

We live now in an age of challenger parties, as they prod and probe the global elite consensus that seems to be annoy so many voters

We have just witnessed an extraordinary series of political events. Once great political parties have willingly collapsed, wedded to policies and views that drive them out of office and out of parliaments, after years of dominance. How and why has this happened? Is the era of Christian Democracy and Social Democracy over?

In 1995 the French presidential election saw the centre left lose office to be replaced by the centre right. The unpopular centre left presidency came to a sad end with the terminal illness of Mr Mitterand. His successor was unable to defeat Mr Chirac, the chosen candidate of the Republicans on the centre right.

This election confirmed the typical post-war pattern. The two main parties, the Republicans and the Socialists, alternated in power depending on their fluctuating fortunes. A range of challenger parties pressed their particular issues but did not break through electorally.

The 1994 German election had confirmed a similar pattern In Germany. There the proportional representation system meant minor parties had a chance to be junior partners in coalition with one or other of the main parties, but the dominance of the Christian Democrats and Social Democrats remained entrenched. The CDU got 37.2% of the vote, with their allies in Bavaria the CSU adding 7.2%. The SPD received 38.3%.

Much of democratic western Europe post 1945 observed a similar pattern. Centre left and centre right dominated elections, and alternated in government. Governments tended to change if there was a recession or other period of poor economic performance.

This led some voters to question their allegiances and to switch votes. Politics was a matter of modest changes of direction.

When a centre right government lost to the centre left there would be moderate tax rises, some increase in public spending programmes and a bit more emphasis on the role of government in the provision of services and people's lives.

When a centre left government lost to the centre right there would be modest tax reductions, a slowing of the rate of growth in public spending and more emphasis on the role of the private sector in fuelling growth and prosperity.

Political strategists argued that the political battle was one for the votes of a limited number of voters who were said to be in the centre, and who were swing voters.

After too long a period of centre left government they would fancy a tax cut and more dynamism in the private sector. After a long period of centre right government they would fancy more emphasis on improving public services by spending more tax money.

First past the post

This pattern was also reflected in the two great Anglo Saxon democracies that had stood together during the second world war.

Both have first past the post systems designed to produce a majority. Both have long standing centre right and centre left parties contesting power.

In the USA the Republicans and Democrats have alternated in Presidential office and in control of the Congress throughout the post-war period. In the UK Labour and the Conservatives have similarly alternated in government, with just three Parliaments where a third party has been a junior coalition partner to produce a majority.

Twentieth century politics was similarly framed to the continent, with strategists urging a tilt to the left for Republicans and Conservative leaderships wanting to win over the middle, and urging Democrats and Labour to genuflect to the right to do the same.

Labour famously argued they were relaxed about people being rich and would keep the top rate of tax down to 40% to win their long period in office from 1997 to 2010. Conservatives have long been dedicated supporters of the NHS providing a near monopoly of all healthcare for the state. Bill Clinton reassured Republicans on their issues just as George Bush tilted towards some Democrat sympathisers.

The motive behind changing a government often stemmed from economic disappointment.

In the world before the Euro national parliaments and presidents still had considerable power to influence economic outturns, and considerable influence over central banks.

In the UK the Conservatives lost office in 1974 after presiding over the oil crash of the early 1970s. Labour lost office after one disastrous parliament where they ran out of money and had to visit the IMF to keep the country afloat.

The Conservatives had a long period of relative economic success, only to throw it away by adopting the damaging ERM, which brought on a recession in 1992-3. They lost heavily in the first election after the damage was revealed, in 1997. Labour stayed in government until 2010, brought down to a heavy defeat by allowing the banking crash and great recession. This history was mirrored elsewhere on the continent and in the USA.

A different century

How different the 21st century is. This comfortable world of two party politics has been ripped apart on the European continent, and has been pressured to change dramatically in the USA and the UK within the old two-party framework.

The French presidential election of April to May 2017 produced two candidates for the second and decisive round of the contest who did not belong to either of the two traditional main parties.

Mr Macron left the socialists where he had been a minister and formed an entirely new movement called En Marche, which swept to an impressive victory with no baggage and not that much defining policy. His rival was Marine Le Pen of the National Front, offering a very different vision of France and her role in the world.

At the base of their dispute was the issue of the EU. Mr Macron favoured more commitment and integration, whilst Ms Le Pen argued for partial disengagement and more national French policy. The two traditional parties had nothing new they wanted to say about this big issue, and were understandably excluded from the conversation.

The German 2017 election also saw a slump in support for the two traditional parties. The SPD managed just 20.5% whilst the CDU only polled 26.8%. The two main parties in Germany between them could not command the support of half the electorate.

Along with their CSU allies the CDU was eventually able to form a grand coalition with their SPD rivals, just edging over the bar of 50% of the vote between the three parties. Since then in opinion polls the SPD has fallen to a mere 14% as people disapprove of its entry into another coalition with its main rival.

Germany is the last bastion of the old system of Christian Democrats versus Socialists on a continent where elsewhere the fortunes of the dominant parties of the previous century has been even more dire. Even in Germany there is now a feeling that the old parties do not meet current needs or engage with current concerns and viewpoints.

The new threats to the old order in Germany come from the left with the upsurge in support for the Greens, and from the right in the form of the AFD party.

This party began as an anti-Euro party, with a group of professors arguing that the currency was unstable without proper financial foundations, and proposing Germany should leave rather than pay the bills to keep the zone together. This never attracted huge support. When the party added to its platform a strong demand to reduce the flow of migrants into Germany support soared.

It now leads opposition in the German parliament, which has changed the political landscape dramatically. Suddenly the issues the old parties did not want discussed are on the agenda, forcing the CDU and SPD to ask themselves more difficult questions about their stance to migration, EU solidarity and EU financing.

Greece shows just how far support for the traditional parties can fall if economic performance remains bad for a long period. In 2009 as the Greek economic collapse was beginning, the centre left main party Pasok polled

43.0% and its principal rival on the centre right, New Democracy, attracted 33.5%.

It proved to be a bitter win for Pasok, who went on in government to preside over a sharp fall in output, incomes and living standards. Today Greek output and income per head is still more than fifth lower than in 2007. In the latest polls Pasok is on around 5%, having scored just 6.3% in the September 2015 election.

The last decade has seen a whirlwind transformation of Greek politics, with the arrival of new party challenger Syriza. Such was the anger and frustration at the economic collapse brought on by traditional politics that Syriza was swept into office rapidly to try to confront the EU and force it to offer Greece a better deal. The party valiantly fought against the endless austerity packages, only to lose when the EU faced Greece with the stark choice of giving in and staying in the Euro, or insisting on a different approach and being forced out in messy circumstances with the banking system badly damaged.

The Greek public and its chosen champion party decided on buckling. Since then Syriza has stayed relatively high in the polls despite defeat by the EU. This is probably in recognition of the way the public, like their chosen party agent, decided they did want to give in. It has also been saved by no new challenger party emerging with better ideas on how to fight off endless recession and austerity.

The Greek tale provides ample evidence that electors become frustrated by economic failure and look for an alternative political party when the main parties no longer offer plausible hope. It also shows that if you wish to remain wedded to the Euro and EU economic system there is not a great deal parties in national government can do to change the outlook.

They have to comply, accepting the budget disciplines and the money policy served up by the European Central Bank. It means that voters can express their frustration by voting for protest parties, or express their wishes on other matters where national government may have some power left. It means much continental politics is now a breeding ground for a vast array of new parties and movements.

The Dutch economy has been one of the few economies in the Eurozone that has performed relatively well under the aegis of EU policy. Despite this, it has still been on a similar political journey.

In the 1989 election in a PR system which encouraged party differentiation and single issue parties, the Christian Democrats still got 35.3% of the vote and their main rival Labour received 31.9% of the vote.

In 2017 the People's party, heir to the centre right, was down to 21.3% whilst 13.1% went to the challenger Party for Freedom on an anti-migration and EU scepticism ticket.

The rest of the vote splintered between many parties with most in single figures only, including a poor performance by the old Labour centre left which polled just 5.7%. In the 2019 senate elections another new anti-migrant party emerged to top the poll and to help push the four-party governing coalition into a minority.

The Italian lesson

In Italy the centre right has been through two main reconstructions this century. The old Christian Democrat party was usurped by Berlusconi's brand of media-led populism for a period. More recently his Forza movement has been nudged out of leadership of the right by the more stridently Eurosceptic Lega.

In the 2018 general election the centre right coalition gained 37%, with Lega edging ahead of Forza. Subsequently Lega has soared in opinion polls at the expense of its coalition partners. Meanwhile Cinque Stelle, a relatively new movement formed originally by a comedian fed up with traditional parties, gained 32.7% of the vote and is now in coalition government with Lega.

The Italian economy has floundered over the last decade, with incomes and output still below 2007 levels. Unemployment remains obstinately high, especially for young people. The traditional parties have stayed wedded to Eurozone austerity policies which are criticised from the tax-cutting Lega side and from the bigger benefits Cinque Stelle side of the argument.

In Spain as recently as 2011 the centre right Partido Popular (PP) won the general election with 44.6% of the vote, with the socialist centre left opposition coming second with 28.8%. By 2016 the PP was down to 33% and the socialists down to 22.6%, with Spain now mired in an era of weak coalition governments struggling from one vote to the next.

Meanwhile Catalan nationalism is strong, electing nationalist representatives to Parliament. Two challenger parties have risen well in the polls, Cuidadanos and Podemos. Both these parties express frustration at traditional politics and policies. Neither adopt the anti-migrant and Eurosceptic rhetoric of the National Front In France or Lega or AFD, and neither have broken through in the way Syriza did in Greece. More recently an anti-migrant populist party called Vox has started to take votes from all the other parties.

It is clear that the two traditional parties in most continental countries have made extraordinary political sacrifices of themselves in the cause of EU integration. They suffered both from the general banking crash and great recession, and from the continuing Euro crises that followed.

Where the Anglo Saxon economies recovered and have living standards above 2007 levels, parts of the Eurozone have stagnated at lower levels than before the crash.

The common feature of the centre left and centre right parties on the continent that have been through similar declines is their stalwart support for the EU system and their reluctance to argue for reform at EU level. They have lacked the ability to work together in the Council of Ministers to change direction, and where they form common alliances in the European Parliament they have endorsed an agenda that is clearly unpopular with their voters back home.

Part of the background is proportional representation which makes parties on the continent more used to coalition and power sharing, but it is not the reason the two main parties in each case have suffered major or catastrophic decline.

In the last century and indeed in many cases up to 2010 the two traditional parties alternated in government, sometimes winning a majority and sometimes as dominant leaders of a coalition under those same PR systems.

The last bastions

Germany and Spain are the last bastions of centre right in government. In Germany they can only do so in alliance with their main old rivals, and in Spain only in a multi-party coalition with no authority.

It is a dramatic change. It shows the power of the EU scheme to dominate those involved. Normally political parties that experience large falls in their support go through radical change and come up with new ideas and new people capable of winning back power.

The two Anglo Saxon great democracies have trodden a different path in recent years.

It did look as if the UK was beginning to experience the same change as the continent, with a decline in support for both Labour and the Conservatives.

In the 2010 election the public clearly signalled they wanted to change from Labour, and gave them just 30% of the vote. They only gave the Conservatives 36%, requiring them to enter a coalition with the Liberal Democrats to govern.

In the following 2015 election the electorate had sufficient confidence in the Conservatives to give them a small majority of seats, but still with a modest 36% of the vote only. The Lib Dems were hammered for breaking their promises particularly over student fees when in government, but other challenger parties including the SNP and Ukip proved popular. The SNP showed that even with a first-past-the-post system for Westminster a challenger party could break through and win a lot of seats.

Sensing that the public mood was shifting over the traditional two-party structure and its offering, the Conservatives in office offered two referendums to ask the people to settle big constitutional issues that were overhanging the debate.

The response to SNP success at the polls was to grant them the one thing they always said they wanted most, a referendum on whether Scotland should become independent of the rest of the UK. The vote was held and the Scottish people decided to stay with the UK. In subsequent elections SNP support started to wane.

And then came the 2016 referendum

The Conservatives also offered a referendum on continued membership of the EU, which helped the party win a majority in 2015. The vote when held resulted in a public decision to leave.

This decision transformed UK politics. Where before the referendum support for the two parties was waning, after the vote Ukip supporters and some Labour supporters who wanted Brexit were willing to transfer their voting allegiance to the Conservatives who appeared to be the party most likely to implement the decision.

Labour too was on a journey, and under a new left radical leader made a more aggressive socialist offering to the public in the 2017 general election whilst also promising to honour the EU referendum result.

In one bound the two main parties had reconnected with more voters. The Conservatives polled 42.4% based on their adherence to Brexit, and Labour polled 40% with their more socialist offering allied to Brexit. The two old parties had adapted to a new mood of radical politics where being in the so called centre did not produce victory, and where backing EU austerity was bad news.

Still two parties in the USA

The USA never looked as if it was going to end the two-party system, which remained strong despite the crash of 2010.

Both parties, however, responded very directly to the new mood which affected the new world as well as the old.

The Democrats fielded Hilary Clinton as their candidate for the 2016 Presidential election. She was the very embodiment of the elite establishment . She oozed entitlement from her eight years as First Lady and service as Secretary of State to President Obama. Her top down website offering told her supporters what she had said and thought without allowing much interaction or showing much sensitivity to the strong new radical currents in US politics.

She thought and hoped her nomination would be a shoo-in, as an obvious candidate who had prepared for years for this opportunity. The USA has a habit of creating political dynasties with apparent inheritance, which is strange in a country founded on rejecting the inheritance principle of kings and princes.

Instead a left-wing radical, Bernie Sanders, dogged her every step to the nomination. In the final tally she scored 55% and he managed a creditable 43%, with the Democrat establishment strongly against him and despite Hilary's access to much more money to campaign.

The Democrat party looked divided, and the delay in getting accepted damaged her position with the wider electorate. It also meant it was more difficult for her to energise the Democrat base to campaign or even in some cases to vote for her, because they liked what they had heard from Bernie Sanders and she was no Bernie Sanders.

The Republican contest turned out to be a one candidate race. I remember tuning in to see some of the early debates as they wrestled for the nomination. They were hilarious. A series of well-groomed and well trained political insiders set out their establishment stalls as to why it should now be their turn to inhabit the White House.

They lacked passion and vision, and were unable to break through with the voters over what they wanted to do for America.

Bashing them from all directions was Donald Trump, revelling in being a political novice or outsider. He broke through with outrageous statements and populist claims. He geared his message to the swing voters in Democrat industrial heartlands that had been let down in recent years and wanted some hope that their jobs might come back or their pay might go up again.

Trump vs the establishment

The political establishment did not know how to react to Mr Trump. They saw they could not control him. He had his own money and had no need to kow tow to their wishes and views, such as they were.

The more they protested against what they saw as being his bad language and offensive remarks, the more he grabbed the headlines and showed he would be different. As I expected, he won the nomination easily and convincingly. The establishment party spent most of the primary campaign trying to decide which of their hopeless candidates they should back to stop Trump, making their whole exercise predictably negative.

Donald Trump secured 44.9% of first instance votes to Ted Cruz's 25.1% with the others struggling to get into double figures. In the final vote he won 70%.

The Republicans took time coming to terms with this re-writing of the elections' book. Enough of them decided it best to co-operate with the winner to help him win the Presidency against arguably the best prepared insider to run, and the first serious woman candidate for the world's top political job. The defeat of Mrs Clinton was a body blow to the elite establishment, who had lost one of their finest from elected office.

The combination of a great recession following the banking crash, and the fashionable tendencies of the elite to welcome and loosely supervise global and EU government has transformed western democratic politics and parties. We live now in an age of challenger parties, as they prod and probe the global elite consensus that seems to be annoy so many voters.

This phenomenon has spread more widely. In Hungary Victor Orban has swept to power with a massive 49.3% vote in the last election giving him considerable scope to follow his Eurosceptic and anti-migrant tendencies. In Poland the new President Duda is also a populist with strong views. In Brazil President Bolsonaro won with 55% of the vote with some Trump like features to his campaign.

We must turn now to look in more detail at the long and close fought struggle between the Euro elite and the pro Brexit forces in the UK, on one of the front lines of this political battle.

Chapter 6

Brexit – the front line of the establishment's battle for control

A fight in which one side did not properly engage was fought and lost. Phoney forecasts, silly scares and arrogant assumptions left a great deal of damage

In early 2016 the pro-EU establishment in the UK was feeling pleased with itself.

They thought granting a referendum to the people on the vexed issue of the UK's membership of the EU should settle the issue once and for all. The polls showed pretty steady leads for Remain.

Big business, the leading global institutions, the President of the USA and most informed commentators would come out for the UK to stay in. A win, any win, in the referendum would seal it.

The government had carefully told the UK people it was a once-in-a-generation opportunity and had tipped the scale in favour of Remain as much as they dare. They would send a leaflet to every home just before the campaign proper so the government could set out just how damaging they thought leaving would be.

They knew the public was a bit unruly on this topic and a few tabloid newspapers liked to make trouble, but they were confident that in the end in the privacy of the polling booth the voters would see sense and see there was no alternative. UK government would then be free to respond much more positively to the EU.

Without the authority of a recent referendum they saw a cramped and ugly debate, making it difficult to get through new EU laws and powers. Eurosceptic MPs would be briefed against as bad losers if they carried on their opposition after a referendum defeat. It would be so much easier to marginalise them once the public had spoken.

Everything the government did on the EU was in the teeth of determined criticism and opposition from within parliament to further transfers of power. In their view it would be such a relief to have the authority of the people behind making the further compromises with EU controls that a grown country needed to make.

Remain decided to run a campaign that remorselessly focused on a few economic issues, mainly to do with future trading once the UK had left.

They decided on a negative campaign, trying to persuade voters that though they might not like the EU, EU trade was important to our jobs and incomes and somehow that trade was at risk if the UK pulled out.

The Remain campaign had all the advantages that incumbency and the elite possess. They could call up plenty of free and powerful support for their case from a galaxy of international bodies, big businesses and overseas governments.

They felt able legally to use the considerable resources of the UK state to churn out negative forecasts for leaving. They set out in great detail a large number of things they though could go wrong if the UK had the temerity to detach itself from EU rules. They should have won if elections can be manipulated by big money and big messaging, and most of the time most of them thought they would win.

The wrong campaign

Unfortunately for them their choice of campaign displayed arrogant mis-judgements that continued to haunt them.

The decision not to defend the EU vision or even to accept that it had a vision of full economic, monetary and political union made them look dishonest and out of touch.

Whilst the continental debate accepts that the cause of the EU is to work towards ever closer union, with countries and commissioners busily taking step after step on the road to a federal government of Europe, the Remain team pretended this was not happening and denied it in most of the debates.

Voters were told there would be no European army as plans proceeded for just that. They were told the UK was not in the Euro and never needed to join the Euro whilst the EU made clear that the Euro is central to the whole project.

The rest of the EU was becoming irritated at the UK's unwillingness for the EU to use the full range of EU institutions, powers and budgets to support the currency. The UK had to be excluded from finance meetings when they turned to Euro matters.

The electorate were told that the EU has no powers over the UK tax system at the same time as the VAT rules prevented parliament removing VAT from products it did not wish to tax, and as successive court cases overrode the view of the UK parliament on what corporate tax we could levy on big business.

Some even tried to claim that as the UK is not part of the Schengen arrangements it therefore did not have to accept free movement of people, yet that policy is a fundamental principle which the UK accepts under treaty law.

They told their audiences the UK could control its own benefits system, yet Prime Minister Cameron in his renegotiation was not even granted the right to increase the length of time someone needed to be living and working in the UK from the continent before they qualified for benefits.

Remain argued that moves towards full union were not going to happen, They wanted people to believe it was all a fiction made up by extreme Eurosceptics. They sought to portray Eurosceptic campaigners as people who had a narrow fixation with the EU, had got it all out of proportion, and were on weak ground when it came to trade and economies.

Remain had over the years succeeded in keeping the Eurosceptic representation in Parliament to around 100 Conservative MPs and a handful of Labour MPs.

The Labour view

Labour had been on a long journey from being a party in the 1980s with many who wanted out, to being a party which went along with the EU scheme as part of modern life.

Whilst many in the party did not share Mr Blair's great enthusiasm for the EU project, most accepted the view that it was best to go along with it. They tried to make out it was just a Conservative issue which split that party but nothing else.

The Remain majorities in successive Parliaments always played down any transfer of power to the EU. They maintained the argument that it was primarily a trading arrangement, and that Eurosceptics were out of touch in always wanting to turn it into a big constitutional issue.

The Remain side before the vote repeatedly tried to stop or play down debate on EU matters, claiming the public was not interested and they issues were of little significance.

When the results of the referendum were known it turned out that Labour had some of the most anti EU constituencies in the country as well as some of the most pro EU places, confirming the way the EU issue split more than one party. Many voters in the referendum did think the constitutional issues mattered a lot and thought the transfer of power had been significant.

Why people like Europe

It is possible to understand the passion some do have for a country called Europe.

This does not mean someone necessarily wants it for the UK. If you invite too many countries into forming such a new nation you make it much more difficult for it to work. Nonetheless it is a bold vision which some will enthuse over.

The Euro was a big step on that journey, and requires more large steps to political union to be made to ensure it works. No-one from Remain in the debates usually shared that vision or was prepared to argue that this is what many on the continent want and are busy creating.

It took away any pretence at vision and left them denying what seemed obvious to many Leave voters, that the EU is about ever closer union. Remain spokesmen and women mirrored the polling which always showed only a small minority of UK voters admired the vision of a politically united Europe and wanted the UK to be part of it.

Remain's decision to turn negative also had its drawbacks. They ran the risk of caricaturing themselves, which they did as the campaign advanced by becoming ever shriller and more extreme in their gloomy predictions.

People often like their politicians to advocate sensible optimism, to show why tomorrow can be better than today. Instead Remain accepted that today wasn't much good, but threatened an even worse tomorrow if people dared to vote Leave.

Remain did not seek to defend the high overall unemployment and high youth unemployment across much of the Eurozone, or the highly bureaucratic style of regulation or the proposed additional EU taxes.

The Treasury and the Bank of England became the motors of the Remain campaign, used by the Chancellor within the rules as he saw them to churn out a vast array of material pointing to bad tomorrows.

The short-term forecast for the period immediately after a Leave vote told the country to expect a recession the next winter, 500,000 or more job losses, rising unemployment, a collapse in house prices and a fall in the pound.

Responding to these Vote Leave dismissed all save the one about the pound. The pound had been falling for sometime within the EU, and had regularly fallen as well as risen during our time in the EU. Vote Leave concluded it would continue both to fall and to rise again once the UK left, as indeed proved to be the case.

As expected after the vote the economy continued to grow at a decent pace, employment continued to rise, house prices did not fall and there was no recession.

Remain and their many supporters in the media made it difficult to sustain an alternative economic view to this crass pessimism by the official sources.

Leave spokesmen were always asked who did they think they were to dare to disagree with the mighty Treasury and the forces of global misinformation from sources like the IMF and World Bank?

These organisations had been so spectacularly wrong about the ERM and the world banking crash, so they had less influence over voters than the Remain campaigners imagined. There was never a hint of humility or irony in the media questions relying on these forecasts, as they just assumed they would be right and Leave would be wrong . They had no wish to revisit past clashes over the banking crash and the ERM where the Remain establishment had been on the wrong side of the argument.

In order to relieve pressure against their unreliable macro view, they often turned to detail about customs checks, standards, licences and the other intricacies of trade.

Leave responded by developing its own expertise on World Trade terms. They researched the figures to confirm that the UK did more trade with non-EU than with EU, most of that was just done under WTO rules, it was faster growing than the EU trade, and was in surplus instead of deficit.

Remain had to deal with a flaw in their reliance on international bodies, because Leave had found one in the form of the WTO on its side. So Remain had to seek to undermine the one international body that was not on its side, which happened to be the most important one for the pursuit of freer trade.

If you run a campaign based on good references from elite institutions it is a problem if one or more of those bodies is out of line.

Leave's different problems

The Leave campaign had different problems to contend with. It all started very badly. The Ukip wing of the loose coalition to leave wanted to major on the issue of freedom of movement and migration.

Conservative and Labour forces for Leave were strongly against this.

The polling showed that the 20% or so support which Ukip could command did indeed worry a lot about immigration and wanted the UK to be able to close its borders to many low-income migrants seeking low-paid jobs and benefit top up in the UK from the continent. It also showed that concentrating on this issue would if anything put off the other 30% needed to win, as their preoccupations were wider.

With strong views on both sides the Leave forces spent the first months of the run up to the referendum battling over whether Leave EU or Vote Leave would be the official campaign.

Leave EU favoured the Ukip approach and was largely Ukip driven. Vote Leave favoured the main party approach and had representatives of Labour and Conservative in prominent positions on its board.

A long and often bitter battle ensued, with the press making much of a house divided. Leave was written off as the predictable losers Remain said it was, endorsed by the polling.

In due course Vote Leave won the nomination to run the official campaign and could begin proper planning and spending to build up its team and determine its key messages.

Sorting out the message proved easy. Dominic Cummins and the research proposed "Take Back Control". It received strong endorsement from the main people supporting the campaign. It summed up everything Brexit is about, and answered every question to a leaver's satisfaction. Whatever the problem, the answer could be we will take back control and adopt a UK solution. It was democratic, positive and active. It offered hope in contrast to the gloom of the Remain propaganda.

There were various other issues to resolve.

Some of the business wing of the Conservative party had over the years favoured deregulation, which would require repeal of various pieces of EU legislation once the UK had left. Some particularly favoured repealing some of the employment protections. The case was put strongly that Leave should recommend keeping all of those on departure, aware of the importance of them to the Labour supporters of Leave.

Many Brexiteers felt strongly that the UK did not want to leave the EU to bid down wages and bid up hours. They wanted to leave the EU to improve people's chances of a well -job. It proved easy to get buy in to the idea that Leave would back EU employment laws.

Not a race to the bottom

Remain kept coming back to the threat of a "race to the bottom", a UK outside the EU ditching protections in pursuit of cheaper prices and lower wages.

Vote Leave was grateful to them for constantly ensuring they had an opportunity to explain they wanted the opposite, and the UK would be free to choose something better once we had left.

One of the possible benefits from leaving would be fewer migrants taking low-paid jobs, ending some of the downwards pressure on wages.

Remain ended up having to defend its enthusiasm for more low-pay migrants to flatter the profits of large multinationals. Leave confined deregulatory enthusiasm after the UK left to getting rid of VAT on items that should not attract it, and on sorting out the damage done to the UK fishing grounds by the dreadful regulations the EU imposed.

The well-rehearsed media interviewers told by Remain to ask what Leave would deregulate always gave up after a couple of examples that did not include a race to any bottom.

The fit between Conservative and Labour within Leave was on the whole a good one. Not only did the two parties agree on what they wanted to leave, but they agreed about the immediate areas for reform once out.

Both sides wanted to spend more of the money saved to boost public services, both wanted to help UK business through import saving and better trading terms with the rest of the world. Conservatives readily adopted Labour's colour for the campaign and got used to red ties and red posters.

There was a common sense that Leave were the outsiders, the ones expected to do badly. Being sneered at by the establishment helped bind the coalition together more readily.

Many within Vote Leave thought they would lose. Many of the people at the top of Vote Leave were in their day jobs part of the very same UK establishment that was bending most of its forces to defeat it.

Many of them allowed the establishment story line to rub off on them. They were playing for a decent defeat, an ability to return to their establishment roles saying well, we gave it a democratic run, but of course the establishment was bound to win.

Obama helps out

Ultimate victory was first helped when President Obama spoke out as part of a glittering array of big figures telling us to vote Remain. It was clearly a bridge too far. One of the establishment's own sensible rules is you do not visibly interfere in an election in a neighbour's country. It was bound to produce the opposite reaction, with many UK voters resenting outside interference at such a high level.

Confidence in Leave winning also swelled the day the Chancellor made his punishment budget announcement.

He wanted voters to believe that the UK would have to raise taxes and cut spending were we foolish enough to vote out. Vote Leave may have got overnight warning from the media and seemed ready to respond. It was very unlikely any Chancellor would do any such thing if the UK voted to leave. Were there to be any loss of confidence in the way they suggested they would need to do the opposite and stimulate the economy.

Various Conservative MPs who wanted Leave to win came out and said they had no intention of voting for any such absurd budget, as there would be no need to either raise taxes or cut spending if the UK left the EU. Indeed, on leaving the UK would save a lot of money in EU contributions which could be used to cut taxes and raise spending, the opposite of the Chancellor's proposal.

By the morning of the official launch, as he launched his policy the Chancellor was on the backfoot when he attempted to threaten the nation with dire consequences if we dared to vote out.

He was asked about all the MPs who refused to support him. It was another good case of silly overreach by Project Fear. About that time Leavers started asking whether Remain also thought Brexit would unleash tempests and plagues, or whether it might lead to war. In the latter Leave was not disappointed, as someone for Remain did allow the media to write some such thing.

The main issues that concerned Leave voters went largely ignored by the mainstream media.

They allowed Remain to dominate the airwaves day after day trying to turn it into a detailed conversation about big business, customs and exports. The media repeated the same old scare stories day after day without ever asking detailed questions about how and why things would go wrong.

When a Leave supporter was allowed on they were interrupted and usually prevented from making a wider and more detailed set of points about how WTO actually worked and how the UK could carry on trading with the EU after we had left.

Car fears

There was the car scare – the industry would move abroad. Various companies during and after the vote announced new investments in the UK but these got largely ignored.

There was the general just-in-time scare – the public was told no JIT could work once the UK was out of the EU. Leave pointed out non UK components form part of JIT processes already without preventing the system working, so why would being out altogether stop them?

Business was never asked but just allowed to assert. There was the ever popular scare that medicines would be prevented from getting into the UK. This was particularly odd as the UK will control its own ports and terms of entry, and can simply carry on allowing easy entry for pre-checked pharmaceuticals from the continent.

What did Leave want to talk about? They wanted to talk about restoring democracy.

This elephant in the room was ignored by most of the establishment interviewers and commentators. They were not interested in the advantages of being able to decide your own taxes, approve your own laws and spend your own money.

Remain and therefore the media did see the potency of the argument that the UK needed to spend the money at home, especially during a period of self-imposed austerity which the EU establishment supported and implemented.

So they only allowed one question on this mighty topic, the question of how much money was at issue.

That figure on the side of a bus

Because Vote Leave in some of its materials and on the side of a bus used the then gross figure of UK contributions without netting off the money the UK got back, Remain made this the issue.

Many Leave spokesmen were always careful to give the net figure as well as defending the gross figure as the official figure, but it meant the interview was often about the number rather than about the principle or about how the UK might spend all that money.

Some in the Leave campaign had argued for only using the net figure. The argument for using the gross was it did mean the interviewers kept coming back to it, reminding people that a large sum was at stake.

Most neutral people listening to the exchanges would have gone for the net not the gross figure. Anyone listening even after the attempted demolition job by Remain would also have understood that we would be better off by a large sum if we just left, assuming all else stayed the same.

What was fascinating during the campaign was seeing how much better an understanding voters had of the sovereignty issue than the elite wished them to have.

There was widespread understanding of the nature of the EU project, with many recognising this was not the common market of the Remain campaign's dreams. There was also a realism or cynicism about the EU's trade and economic offer, with many thinking it was designed to help them more than the UK.

There was general resentment at the way our fishing and farming industries had been treated, at the disadvantageous financial settlement, and the bully tactics often used to put through taxes and laws that people did not like.

The fact that Remain had not used their 45 years of bliss in the EU to explain its advantages to the public set them up for a fall when it came to Judgement Day.

Voters remembered the big decline in the fishing industry, the banning of UK beef, the long arguments about the substantial financial contributions and the parliamentary battles over each successive treaty and the powers it transferred to the continent.

A bolt from the blue

The result of the referendum came as a bolt from the blue for the establishment.

The BBC cancelled or shortened interviews planned with Eurosceptics, as they had been invited to portray them in defeat, not in victory. Instead of taking defeat well many Remain media outlets, politicians and campaigners carried on pouring out their negative materials about Brexit as if they were still fighting the referendum.

It never occurred to them that maybe it was the whole tenor of their negative campaign that had contributed to their downfall. Indeed, to this day many have carried on trying to derail Brexit and are now pushing for a second referendum on the same issue.

They are scornful of all who voted Leave, and believe if voters were made to do it again they would repent and see it their way. Gone are the fine words before the vote that the people would decide in a once in a generation vote. No-one for one moment thinks they would have offered Leave a second shot if they had lost.

The idea that the UK needs a second referendum is a curious development. The forces of Remain and the EU recognise the ultimate sovereignty of the people, so they see that if they are to have their way and keep the UK in the EU there needs to an official reversal of the verdict in the vote.

Their problem is in deciding what the question should be and in persuading enough people and MPs that this is now a necessity.

Some in the Remain camp favour a three-way vote. They say the country now knows more about leaving than in the original debate. They want the public to decide whether to accept the withdrawal agreement offered by the EU and the further 21 to 45 months of talks about a future partnership, or to stay in the EU by cancelling the Article 50 notification of departure, or to leave with no agreement.

There are several problems with this approach.

The first is the winning proposal might only attract 34% support, leaving almost two thirds of the public angry or unhappy about the outcome.

The second is the establishment proposal of signing the withdrawal agreement leaves the country with many more months of uncertainty and no knowledge of what leave will then looks like as all rests to be agreed after the event.

Other advocates of the second vote split between the pro EU variant, where the country would decide between Remain and the managed partial exit under the withdrawal agreement, and those who simply want to re-run Remain against Leave with no withdrawal agreement.

The first of these effectively disenfranchises the majority who voted Leave, as there is no proper Leave option on the ballot paper. The second leads many voters to ask why they have to do it all again, as they meant what they voted the first time round. It looks arrogant to say to voters they did not know what they were doing and need to think again.

Most supporters of a second referendum are Remain voters who wish to reverse the decision. The overwhelming majority of Leave voters are happy with their choice and frustrated at the delay in implementing it. Their most common phrase in response is "Just get on with it".

The establishment's attempts have been intense to dilute or cancel Brexit. They never made a passionate or honest case for membership all the time the UK was in it. They always played down the more visionary parts of it, or made sure the UK was opted out of them for fear of public retribution. Now membership is to be taken away, they still lecture the country on the mistake the majority made in their view. The Leave voters are busily saying to Remain, "We still don't believe you".

The establishment lost a battle which it did not properly engage in. Its phoney forecasts, silly scares and arrogant assumption it would it win have left it damaged.

Leave remains anxious that somehow even at the last minute it will be cheated from its determination to rebuild an accountable democracy in the UK. This remains one of the most intense battles between the elite and the populists.

Chapter 7

Elite media vs social media – and the battle over fake news

Populists feel they are being lied to by governments and by governments' associates in the press and broadcasters

The rise of populist movements take place at a time of dramatic change in the world of the media.

The 20th century saw the rise of mass media through radio and television providing a homogenous product for the many. It was top down, with an elite deciding the stories for the news, the programmes for entertainment and education, and the views that could be transmitted.

There was a public censorship to avoid libel and preserve good taste. There was also an unseen censorship that regarded some views and controversies as beyond the pale for broadcasting.

The BBC with its high ideals of the Reithian era could seem condescending to some, but was diligent in presenting its own ideas of material that was educational and informative.

The media class exercised considerable control over content and the national debate, and helped frame the news. Individuals had to watch or listen to what was served up when it was broadcast. They had the choice to respond to the programmes provided after they had been transmitted, or to avoid listening and watching when the output was strongly against their views and interests.

The first technological breach in this system of them and us, broadcaster and audience, came with the video recorder allowing people to time shift the broadcast programmes. This allowed an individual to skip the programmes available on any given night, and watch something originally broadcast at another time more to their taste.

The advent of more competitive independent channels also gave the audience more variety, with commercial stations having to tailor their content more to the views and interests of their audience.

The US model with a larger number of competitive commercial channels spawned programmes with different outlooks and offerings. This gave individuals more choice than the state or monopoly systems in some other countries. The US system, however, was still largely top down, with the competitor companies often sharing a common view of what was news and what was entertainment. It gradually evolved to create channels that pushed a particular viewpoint.

A revolution with unknown consequences

In the current century there has been a revolution in media where the consequences are still being worked through and thought out.

The mobile phone and tablet computer double up as video and still cameras. Most people most of the time now have a camera handy, so they can capture events and news as it happens before the conventional media crews arrive with professional equipment.

The media outlets are often forced to adopt or seek out amateur footage of events when they catch on to a story. News stories may run first on social media, with many people becoming their own editor and publisher.

If someone wishes to share a moment, an idea, an event with others they can do so almost instantaneously through a platform like Facebook. If others like it or think it interesting it will take off and be widely shared whether the media barons think it a story or not.

The task of reporting is democratised, and can become enmeshed with the task of inviting people to events or protests. If someone who supports a political march puts the details out on social media, it is a kind of advertising of the event.

If they then film some of it as it happens and put that out they are both trying to attract more people to join and acting as journalists covering the march as it occurs. The conventional media may have their own wish not to cover a particular event, but social media can bypass them. If the social media output gets a lot of traction the media are then usually forced into covering it to so they do not seem too out of touch.

Social media grew rapidly in the early years of the current century, as the digital revolution made access easy and more widespread.

The wide adoption of tablets and smart phones means billions of people worldwide can access social media sites. Most of the sites adopted a business model where use of the site is free to the user.

The reward to the provider comes from advertising revenues. The more a social media site is used, the more it can charge advertisers for its use.

Many people now like the freedom they can enjoy, sharing news and entertainment they like and think is relevant to them. It is particularly liked by those who wish to develop a cause or group. They have reach to all users of a large social network site. They can set out what they are trying to do and how they are doing it. They then attract likeminded people to form a group on social media. This group can then pump out news and views to seek to win more to their cause.

The world of politics has been much changed by these technological and social developments.

What Obama did...

Candidate Obama seeking the presidency used websites and emails to great effect. Using email lists and signing people up to a website enabled him to crowd fund much of his campaign, preferring small donations from many people rather than larger donations from a few.

His team helped him make the messages of the emails more unashamedly about the individuals receiving them, rather than being just top-down messages from the candidate.

This had a double advantage. Many people were more interested in themselves than in a politician writing to them. It meant as well there was no need to define the candidate's views or policies too sharply, to avoid upsetting people they were seeking to engage.

It was very noteworthy, however, that once he had gained the presidency this style ended, as there was a day of reckoning once in power. He literally campaigned in the poetry of social media, and governed in the prose of official statements and exhortations to supporters. He could rise on policy light, but he could not govern on policy light.

He had, of course, set out policy positions during the campaign, though often not stressing them in the emails to possible supporters. After his election he found it difficult to keep a few of his prominent pledges. He failed to close down Guantanamo Bay, perhaps the best known of his promises. He struggled with health care reform and finally got it through at large political cost.

...and what Trump did

Donald Trump became the poster boy of the next generation of technology by using the Twittersphere.

Where a blog based campaign could handle paragraphs, developed policies and more sophisticated issues, Twitter can only handle sound-bite-sized policy or attitudes.

It is a great means to grab attention, to say dramatic things, to send signals about the direction you wish to go in or what you think is wrong. It does not permit more considered and thought through proposals to be set out sensibly.

Mr Trump early on as a potential presidential candidate was persuaded of the potency of this medium. As a political outsider in a hurry he was able to send out a blizzard of messages built around a few key themes in his campaign.

He wanted to make America great again. He wanted to tackle the abuses of trading as he saw it by the Chinese, Germans and Mexicans. He wanted to stand up for more jobs for Americans and more things to be made again in the USA. He wanted to stop excessive immigration and thought extending the border wall with Mexico would help.

He and his advisers boiled this all down to pithy and often contentious tweets which soon gained great traction setting out his stall.

The conventional media largely disliked Mr Trump. The feeling was mutual. He accused them of putting out fake news, which came to mean more or less any anti Trump news, whether true or false.

Meanwhile the conventional media levied the charge of fake news against social media. They identified cases where people made things up and circulated them as true to damage opponents or to strengthen a campaign or to play to the prejudices of people the author wanted to keep on side.

The media complained that social media did not have to operate under the same rules as they did. They refused to be drawn into a role as editors. They declined to check out the authenticity and accuracy of things reported on their websites. They claimed to be outside the law of libel as they were just supplying platforms for others to use and post.

The greater flexibility of the social media meant it was possible to circulate rumours or lies about individuals and institutions without having to check them out, put them to the victim or defend them legally.

As social media grew in scale and scope so gradually lawmakers made them bend somewhat to the conventions and reality of the conventional media. Social websites could not be used to promulgate terrorism, incite people to violence or organise illegal activities.

Wide-ranging laws against money laundering and fraud could include the actions of social media sites allowing or assisting criminals to pursue their criminal aims and could be used to discipline the social media providers. Libel actions also began to move into social media spaces.

An intense battle

The social media battle was particularly intense for the US 2016 presidential election.

At the same time as Donald Trump was proving a master of the new art of tweeting for political gain, his enemies were using social media to circulate lies, allegations and reminders of past bad conduct by him.

There were also allegations that Russian computer experts were intervening in the US election on his side. These have subsequently been dismissed by the Mueller Inquiry into alleged collaboration with Russia.

There were disobliging social media stories circulating both for and against Donald Trump, and some may well have been computer generated. The advent of bots, computers that can repeat and generate messages and ascribe persons to their publication, added a new dimension to the noise of an election.

The conventional US media continued in a more normal way, with pro and anti-Trump titles and programmes. The so-called liberal media was pretty unpleasant throughout about Donald Trump, regarding him as unfit for office and looking forward to his impeachment almost from the day of his election.

Some of the coarse extremes of social media seemed to be rubbing off on a conventional media trying to compete. Increasingly the old media draw on stories and waves of opinion they pick up from social media. Individual critics made up stories to put people off voting for Donald Trump, seeking to portray Trump voters in a bad light.

The populists dislike the whole bias of the conventional media.

They see it as liberal in a bad sense from their point of view. They see it as the corporate arm of global government. They see it as an anti-democratic force seeking to ensure government of the experts by the experts for the experts. They dislike its pro migration, anti-global warming, pro international rules and institutions approach to governing.

They feel it is out to belittle them, to disenfranchise them, to remove their influence and marginalise their role in democratic politics. The media serves up the view of the elite that you can have any policy you like as long as it is the one the media and the experts have set out.

The role of the BBC

The question of experts lies behind much of this battle.

It is particularly stark in the case of the BBC and the UK. The US has some choice of channels with some channels Republican oriented and some pro the Democrats, and has experts on TV who have to declare who they vote for. In contrast the UK has a dominant state broadcaster which seeks to deny experts have political views and emotional prejudices.

The BBC is established under its 1926 founding charter. This requires the Corporation to be "independent". "The mission of the BBC is to act in the public interest, serving all audiences through the provision of impartial high quality and distinctive output and services which inform, educate and entertain".

That sounds great, and implies balance and catering for a wide range of political and social views. They have a particular duty to put out "accurate and impartial news" and to reflect "the different cultures and alternative viewpoints that make up its society". This has proved an impossible task for a nation that has been substantially Eurosceptic for many years, and has voted to leave the EU.

The BBC has long had a different approach to the EU from the majority view in the referendum.

Various studies have shown how the BBC has interviewed countless more pro EU people than anti EU commentators over the years of our membership.

They have interrupted and criticised and denigrated the sceptics but usually allowed the pro Europeans to say what they want without interruption and often with agreement from the interviewers.

The BBC has been a keen exponent of climate change theory, has given considerable and often favourable airtime to green experts, has failed to criticise the ERM or to tackle the run up to the banking crash by putting alternative views sufficiently. On all the things the populists worry about the BBC seems to them to have an official line hostile to them, their views and their causes.

One of the causes of tension is the way the BBC treats experts.

They are introduced in a positive way and interviewed with a reverence that contrasts sharply with the hectoring and disbelieving style of interviewing adopted for politicians, especially for ones who do not take the establishment line on issues.

The expert is assumed to be politically neutral and representative of their profession or specialism even when they may be partisan and part of a faction within their area of interest. They are rarely asked about their past successes and failures at predicting even though they are often wanted to venture some forecast about the future. Nor are they asked about who disagrees with them.

Rarely do the interviewers press them to explain their positions or seek to challenge them with a different expert view. The whole operation is designed to present to the public the expert's view as the independent truth. This can then be contrasted with politicians who are by definition thought to be pushing a line which people should be wary of.

The use of experts in this way has been most pronounced for two of the main causes of tension between the BBC and a big part of its UK audience.

Economic experts have been deployed to follow the Bank, Treasury and EU line over the ERM, the banking crash and the Euro. Experts who have correctly forecast the bad out turns from these devices and ways of thinking were largely kept off the airwaves or were treated to the political style of interviewing, being grilled as to how they dared face down the consensus view. Once the consensus proved to be wrong the BBC quietly forgot that and did not invite on those who had been right to ask them what might happen next, in case we still disagreed with the consensus.

The BBC has long been a believer and prime propagandist for the anti-global warming lobby, favouring not merely its understanding of the science, which is not particularly contentious, but also its remedies and forecasts which have their critics.

Programme after programme has global warming issues introduced into them with no right of reply for anyone who may have reasons to disagree with some part of the message.

Questions never asked

Climate experts are never asked why past forecasts have gone wrong, or to explain why there were long periods of warming and cooling before mankind was involved and before industrialisation greatly increased man-made carbon dioxide levels.

They rarely discuss water vapour, the role of clouds, the sun's cycle or the other influences on temperature. Nor do they examine specific policies to cut man-made carbon dioxide closely to see if overall they do do this, and to ask if they have other side effects that could be damaging.

There was little worry expressed about the switch to diesels when that was a fashionable way to raise fuel efficiency and therefore cut carbon dioxide emissions. The doubts only set in after stories of fiddles in some manufacturers' figures and second thoughts by legislators about particulates and other exhaust content.

Despite the sustained efforts at getting this message across a large number of people remain unconvinced that the polar ice will all melt and that a two degree temperature rise is a certainty with very damaging effects.

There seems to be some resentment that the matter is never exposed to tough debate and criticism. It is a good example of an issue which exercises the elites but does not come from populist voters who want cheaper energy and like to use their cars.

***

The British public reacted in a flippant way when the UK government asked for a public view of what name to give an Artic explorer ship. The runaway winner of the consultation was Boaty Macboatface.

I quite understand why the government felt they had to override the consultation and choose what they saw as a more appropriate name. I guess the public voted like this because they did not take the consultation seriously and in some way thought it patronising for the government to ask them about this detail of a pet project they had already paid for in taxes.

The government decided to name the vessel after Sir David Attenborough instead, a BBC television employee turned freelance film producer, who is well known for his portraits of nature.

He is generally well thought of thanks to good features on interesting plants, animals and habitats around the globe. The UK love of animals rubs off on anyone who makes friendly movies about them.

Sir David is also a keen advocate of anti-global warming policies, and a critic of Brexit. Government switched from the facetious popular choice to a true insider who has the advantage of being associated with some good nature films.

Michael Gove got into trouble in the referendum campaign by lashing out against experts. The establishment was hurt by one of its own, an accomplished Times journalist turned cabinet minister, daring to query the right of experts to dictate to governments and to public opinion what should happen next.

It is one of the main features of modern government that most annoys the populists. There are some great experts. Of course in a democracy we mainly elect generalists to make the ultimate decisions for us as ministers. If they are sensible they will listen carefully to the experts before making a decision.

Quite often they will decide the weight of expert opinion is strongly in favour of one course and it is best to rely on it. In a minority of cases the minister may need to be brave and say to the experts that he or she has other reasons to come to different conclusion.

These may be based on commonsense or on the popular will, which does not always like what experts want. There are in practice a lot of occasions when the experts disagree and the minister needs to hear conflicting experts. All too often in modern government, and especially in the EU, expertise is channelled into a single opinion, with rival expert views edited out to avoid political power asserting itself or to avoid disagreements that are difficult to resolve, particularly in multi-country institutions.

Irritating politicians

The international system finds handling powerful politicians who disagree with the consensus or the "world order" difficult and irritating. There is a strong pressure to get new leaders to conform.

Most buy into the consensus on austerity, climate change, migration and the rest. If they do not there is a concerted effort to use the conventional media to destabilise them and to undermine their popularity.

Social media makes it more of a two-way conversation. Populist leaders discover through the alternative media that they have many followers for an anti-establishment line. Alternative media also allows other genuine experts who are denied access to the establishment institutions because they disagree to be heard by those who want to listen. It also allows a wide range of hoaxes, false expertise and bogus claims to be made as well.

One of the reasons populism is sweeping through many political firmaments is the growing disillusion with the experts the conventional media serves up, and with the story line they put forward.

Many populist voters disagree that global warming is the biggest problem the world faces. They dislike austerity economics, are scornful of the experts who presided over the banking crash without foreseeing it. They feel they are being lied to by governments and by governments' associates in the media. These groups call themselves the grown ups in global policy and scorn the public. That's why the public hits back in the ballot box, and often say to the elite "We do not believe you".

Chapter 8

Why some people do not want to be citizens of the world or the EU

The populist backlash to the elite's attempt to redefine people's identities

Identity is one of the most explosive forces in politics. People have a sense of place and of belonging. They have a cultural and religious background which bears on who they think they are. Politicians and governments meddle with it or seek to change at their peril.

At the very time when the peoples of Europe have been expressing a view if anything that they wish to be governed and considered in smaller areas or nations, the elite in Europe has been trying to shepherd them into a much bigger union at EU level.

The 20th century saw the break up of previous large trans national governments:

- The first world war saw the end of the Habsburg empire in central Europe.
- The two world wars put an end to any idea of a German centred united Europe.
- The break up of the Soviet Union after its reign of enforced control and terror saw the re-emergence of many smaller countries in eastern Europe. The Czechs decided to split from the Slovaks.
- The Balkans splintered into several states.
- Colonial empires run by European countries in Asia, Africa and Latin America broke up with people wanting to live in their own self-governing countries.

The EU ignored this obvious trend and decided on the goal of ultimate full economic, monetary and political union.

In the early days to help achieve it the Commission took delight in proposing a Europe of the Regions.

The EU set about wooing the regional governments of the member countries with increased devolved powers under EU programmes, and with payments to support regional government projects and initiatives. They reckoned that by appealing to a layer of government two beneath their own they would find ready allies against the powers of the national governments of the member states.

In some cases, as in Germany or Italy, they were responding to a definite regional pattern of loyalties and sympathies. Both these large EU countries had been relatively recently unified as nation states in the 19th century, and still had a substantial apparatus of regional government.

In France and the UK it was a bit different, with much longer experience of centralised national government and expression, and with large capital cities that provided a natural focus of government and leadership for the country as a whole.

Spain was somewhere between the two models. It had been loosely united for longer than Germany or Italy, but had allowed the divisions between the old kingdoms of Catalonia, Leon, Castille and the others to persist in the constitutional architecture. In the cases of the Basque region and Catalonia there are independence movements.

A successful appeal

The appeal to regional governments was relatively successful. In due course, when the EU's power had expanded mightily through successive treaty grants of additional authority, the EU became less concerned to use the regions against the nations, and more concerned about some of the forces destructive of any central power that they had helped foster in their early years.

There had always been a wish by the Flemish and the Walloons of Belgium to pull apart from each other. In Spain Catalonia was never happy as part of the Spanish state, as the richest region within the Spanish union.

In Germany Brandenburg Prussia is different in culture and outlook to western Germany. It was split from West Germany for the post war years of Iron curtain and USSR influence.

In the UK there was a nascent Scottish independence movement, whilst Northern Ireland had for many years been divided over its future between Unionists strongly attached to the UK union and Republicans who wanted an all-Ireland solution.

In Italy the North and the South have important differences, with some strength in northern independence movements in the Veneto and the wider Padania. The EU played a dangerous game in helping stir some of these longer term disputes and hesitations about identity.

Regionalism in the UK

In the United Kingdom the EU encouraged Scottish, Welsh and Irish nationalism but sought to deny the very existence of the largest country within the Union, England.

Successive EU maps refused to include England as an entity. Successive programmes to pay money and encourage projects also ignored England, preferring to create artificial English regions alongside their insistence on treating Scotland as a separate jurisdiction.

England was unified as country more than a thousand years ago, and has a distinguished history and separate culture to the continent. There is little support for carving England up into artificial regions and imposing a system of German-style lander governments on them.

People in Plymouth do not want to be governed from Exeter in some SW Peninsula region, nor do either Plymouth or Exeter relish the idea of being governed from Bristol in some large South Western region.

Liverpool would not take kindly to being governed as part of the North West from Manchester, nor Sunderland as part of the North East from Newcastle. Local city rivalries are an important part of the culture. All accept the supremacy of London as the true capital of England as well as of the UK.

The EU's intervention gave some help to the cause of Scottish nationalism, allowing the nationalist party to claim they wanted an independent Scotland that would look to the EU for all the big brother support and policies they felt a small state would require.

The EU approach to regional government helped them create a more plausible case of what independence would like, which allowed them to build their position over devolution.

Labour was always sympathetic to the idea of a devolved parliament for Scotland, wrongly thinking this would end rather than foster separatist sentiment. The SNP, the nationalist party, proved them wrong by increasing their support and seats in the Scottish Parliament once it had been established by the new Labour government after 1997.

The Scottish Parliament was set up by Labour with a system of proportional representation to make it very difficult or impossible for the SNP to win an outright victory. Indeed Labour was so used to winning most of the Westminster seats in general elections in Scotland they assumed they would remain the dominant political force.

Instead the SNP proved astute at exploiting grievances and making a negative case about UK government until they reached the point where they did indeed win an outright majority of the seats in the Scottish Parliament. They also went on to break through in Westminster elections.

The political pressure for independence created by electoral success at both levels of government led the UK government and Parliament to grant Scotland a referendum on whether voters wished to become independent.

As an English supporter of the Union I thought this was the right approach. I do not want pressed voters in the UK union, If a significant part of the UK wishes to leave they should be given the opportunity to do so in a democratic and orderly way. I also agreed it should be an asymmetric decision. Scotland could decide if she wanted to stay but the rest of the Union would have no say and would accept her decision.

The battle between the Independence movement and the Better Together campaign was long and hard fought.

Better Together did a bit too much on possible negatives if Scotland left for my liking. It turned out however that many Scottish voters wished to stay with the pound and the UK single market.

I agreed with the government view that if Scotland left the union she had to leave the currency.

How can you have an independent budget and tax system if you share a currency? How would you unravel the joint budget without also damaging the system of transfer payments and banking transfers that underpin the single currency?

Enough Scottish voters worried about losing the pound and other features of the union, resulting in a 55% vote to stay in the UK.

The Independence campaign did not offer true independence, claiming rather stupidly that Scotland would be able to stay in the pound and other features of the UK economic union, whilst also stressing their wish to be under EU control in many respects.

In the end it was a kind of grossed up devolution that lost the referendum, as the Independence side reckoned true independence would be even more unpopular with voters. If I were a Scottish nationalist or English nationalist rather than a UK unionist I would want the separating country to be truly independent with its own currency.

A less happy Catalonia

The position in Catalonia was altogether less happy and much less democratic.

Catalan nationalists had followed a similar path to Scottish nationalists, pushing for more and more regional government power. Obtaining more power they thought would relax more voters about their ability to handle it at regional level, as they demonstrated an ability to run a devolved Parliament and administration.

As in Scotland the amount of power granted was never sufficient to satiate wishes for independence. It was always possible to blame the national government for imperfections in Scottish or Catalan government, whoever was really to blame.

The Catalan Parliament and government gained substantial legislative and budgetary powers, and parties in favour of complete independence flourished in this climate. Unlike the UK state the Spanish state refused to accept the verdict of voters by granting an Independence referendum to see if people were voting for Independence parties because they wanted independence rather than as protest and a wish to have more delegated power locally.

Things came to ahead towards the end of 2017. A frustrated Catalan Parliament with a majority in favour of independence held an unauthorised referendum in the absence of the Spanish Parliament agreeing to hold a formal vote.

The decision of the Catalan people to go independent was not recognised nationally, and led to bitterness and recriminations. The nationalist leaderships decided on a debate and a vote in the Catalan Parliament to implement the decision of the referendum, without the consent of the Spanish state which was needed under the constitution.

Meanwhile an angry Spanish state threatened them with punitive action if they dared to circumvent the national constitution and declare independence based on the mandate of the legal Catalan elections and the illegal independence referendum.

Catalonia remained a province of Spain under Spanish law. The ability to determine independence or other constitutional change rested legally with the Spanish national Parliament and government.

A gripping drama followed. The Catalan nationalists claimed a mandate from the wishes of the people as expressed in the ballot box. The Spanish state took a narrow and firm legal view, claiming the referendum was illegal and therefore a misappropriation of public funds.

There was a moment when the world held its breath as to which authority, Catalan or Spanish, the police would obey. The nationalists recognised the strength of the Spanish state's enforcement powers. The leaders fled the country under threat of arrest and prosecution for treason and or for misappropriation of funds and or related alleged crimes.

The EU had to wrestle with the demands from Spain to use EU arrest warrants to send these political leaders back to Spain for trial.

Was this happening in Europe?

It was difficult to believe these things could be happening in a civilised advanced democracy under the aegis of the European Union, yet they were.

It was such a stark contrast to the democratic UK way, where the wishes of the people as expressed in elections to a regional parliament were taken seriously by the union government allowing a proper and legal test of support for independence.

The UK constitution like the Spanish one left the matter of the constitution and referendums as a union power, so the UK could have taken a strict legal view and blocked the aims of the SNP.

I am glad they did not. When a region with a strong sense of its own identity elects a majority of people who want independence the democratic thing to do is to test opinion legally and formally in an independence referendum.

This is not something that should be done too often, as referendums are divisive and distract from day to day concerns and government. They are however essential if a strong pressure of opinion has built up for constitutional change and has not been put to a specific vote for many years.

***

The question of identity has come to dominate or influence politics heavily in many parts of the world.

In the USA Donald Trump took as his winning slogan "Let's make America great again". He deliberately positioned this slogan as a pitch to patriotic Americans who felt as he does that world institutions, foreign governments and economic systems and consensus global politics based on international treaties were somehow getting in the way of the USA's true interests.

He railed against the United Nations, the Nafta trade agreement, the climate change treaties and the unfairness of Nato. There was no major international body or agreement that the elite felt was safe from his gaze and his tweets.

The intense dislike for Mr Trump expressed by many members of the global elite reflected their concern that a Trump presidency might unilaterally withdraw the USA from international agreements and bodies, and might act as a rallying point for all the critics of the global consensus.

In office Mr Trump kept to his word in trying to reform international agreements, or in pulling the USA out of arrangements he felt were one sided or undesirable.

He forced a renegotiation of Nafta, seeking deals with Mexico and Canada separately to reflect his distaste for multi-country agreements. The resulting compromise was a renamed agreement between the three countries with some changes of terms that the USA wanted, but no overall demolition of the NAFTA framework.

He refused to participate in the global talks to firm up actions to tackle excess manmade carbon dioxide, seeing this as a needless attack on US energy policy. Instead he backed further exploitation of oil and gas in the USA, regarding cheaper energy and US self-sufficiency as more important goals than reducing carbon dioxide emissions.

He told his voting base he was putting US jobs and opportunities first by backing the US energy industries. He fell short of breaking up Nato but did put a lot of pressure on the richer Nato members who were failing to contribute even the 2% of GDP minimum to defence spending to mend their ways.

In trade generally he used remedies under the World Trade Organisation. He also used US legislation to take unilateral action against countries he thought were trade cheats as he felt WTO remedies took too long and did not address all of the iniquities he saw.

The world slowly got used to a US president who instead of wanting to lead global bodies wanted to go round them or who saw them as an obstacle to US interests.

A divided USA

These actions reflected deep divisions in US society.

The Democrat half of the nation largely dislike this approach and want a USA which works within global norms and through global institutions.

Hillary Clinton was the perfect advocate of such an approach, used to easy access to these world bodies and sharing many of the preconceptions of the global quangos.

Mr Trump never has much time for the European Union. He is a keen supporter of the UK leaving the EU and has made some wry comments on the lack of enthusiasm for a tough negotiation by the UK government.

He likes offering the opposite to his predecessor President Obama. Mr Obama had allowed himself to be used in the UK referendum campaign as a supporter of Remain, in an unusual intervention in another democratic country's politics. Mr Trump took the opposite view as a man generally sceptical about international bodies. He offered the post-referendum UK government an early trade treaty with the USA, as Mr Obama had opined that the USA would deliberately delay a trade treaty with the UK were the country to leave the EU.

President Trump then despaired of the UK government's tardiness in response. He pointed out how were the UK to sign the withdrawal agreement the EU wanted it would make a US trade treaty difficult as it limits the UK's ability to run an independent trade and regulatory policy.

The anti-Brexit forces in the UK increased their dislike of Mr Trump for daring to offer a helping hand to the UK if it was determined to be independent. The UK government wavered over how close they should be to a US president who did not follow EU and global norms of behaviour and comment.

Elsewhere in the world countries were getting on with the task of splitting themselves into governing territories that better reflected the emotional ties of the people living there.

Eastern Europe separates

The Czech and Slovak republics split themselves up amicably and willingly as soon as they were freed from the Soviet Union. They demonstrated that with political will it was possible to undertake such a complex task in just six months, with most people happier after the divorce was complete.

Bosnia, Serbia, Croatia, Slovenia, Montenegro and Macedonia emerged from the stultifying controls of the Soviet Union, though the births of separate countries only happened after painful wars with some foreign intervention.

The break up of Yugoslavia was bitter, with Kosovo still resting as an autonomous region without international recognition as a separate country.

The break up of the Soviet empire soon ushered in a series of independent states who all wanted to leave the rouble and set up their own currencies. It demonstrated that again where there is political will it is possible to unravel deeply integrated government, and to establish new systems and arrangements in a speedy and effective way.

Where a unified will by all sides was missing in Yugoslavia it was a very painful and long lasting torture to achieve a new settlement. The eventual result was more countries, reflecting the local nature of cultures and sense of identity.

All the economies coming out of the Soviet Union went on to achieve substantial gains in living standards whilst undergoing dramatic transformations from top-down nationalised economies under a Moscow-led currency and banking system.

The problem of identity has been compounded by the large-scale migrations that have ruffled domestic politics in many advanced countries.

Those on the globalist side of the debate welcome these changes, campaign for tolerance and diversity and see the movement of people as wholly positive both for the migrants and for the receiving countries. As we have seen, other more conservative forces worry about the change to national character and attitudes too rapid a migration may cause, and seek deeper levels of integration for the new arrivals. This too is a complex part of the clash of the populists against the establishments.

Globalisation is a mighty economic movement, as well as a preference of the elite.

People of all political views in practice in their daily lives promote trade and commerce globalisation. Now through the world of social media and international large media companies they also enjoy features of a global culture.

This teems with ironies and contradictions. Left-wing radicals who hate global capitalism often want the latest trainer brand or wish to watch a US movie, whilst condemning the system that delivers them. Conservatives who want to put America first or wish the UK to leave the EU do not usually want to cut themselves off from the best products and best value services the world has to offer.

Within parties and movements a struggle is going on to strike the right balance between change and continuity, between migration and controls on movement, between home production and imported product.

What lies at the bottom of the dispute between the elites and the populists is more a question of who makes the decisions. The democratic forces are not saying "No" to all migration, or "No" to all imports. They are saying they want to be more in control. When the elites say adopting global citizenship is best, they reply "We don't believe you".

Chapter 9

Populist dislike of Middle Eastern wars

There is a fundamental disagreement about how best to keep America and Europe safe

Tuesday 11 September 2001 changed the world.

That morning four US airliners were hijacked. Two were flown with all their passengers into the twin towers of the World Trade Centre in New York. One was flown into the Pentagon building. One ended up in a field when the captive passengers heroically saved many lives in Washington by forcing a crash before the intended target in the centre of the US capital. Some 2996 people were killed, and others died afterwards from conditions that may have resulted from the disaster.

The world watched in stunned horror at the endlessly repeated bits of film showing the collision of the jets with the World Trade Centre. The global superpower had a new effective enemy prepared to use asymmetric warfare to do great damage to people, property and national pride. That day most of us in the world mourned with America and felt great sympathy with them in their time of tragedy.

President Bush spoke for many in his nation when he determined that the ultimate culprits behind the dead terrorists on the planes must be brought to justice.

Afghanistan was thought to be harbouring Al Qaeda leaders who were behind the attack. The government of that country was unable or unwilling to hand over Bin Laden, the leader of All Qaeda, to American justice. Instead the USA swiftly marshalled an invasion force with her most immediate allies – the UK, Canada and Australia – launching Operation Enduring Freedom. A long and gruelling series of Middle Eastern wars commenced, with varied western military involvement.

These Middle Eastern wars were to change much.

Starting with the unity that high moral purpose and a wish to avenge a great wrong can bring, they became increasingly contentious at home and abroad.

Electorates on both sides of the Atlantic grew to questioning their purpose and legality the longer they went on. There were worries that they did not succeed in building new democratic nations in the Middle East that could prevent or control terrorist forces from within.

All the Nato allies became involved in some of the military activities. Everywhere questions were raised about the purpose of the interventions, the aftermath of military activity and the moral basis for them.

The reasons the attack on the Twin Towers made such a difference was twofold.

The scale of the operation was immense. If the fourth plane had crashed into the White House or some centrally placed strategic building in Washington the damage would have been even greater.

The attack highlighted a new vulnerability for the USA which few had suspected. The world's greatest armed forces that no other power could hope to defeat, and the oceans that surround the USA keeping it from most of its enemies, were no protection against a handful of evil individuals prepared to think big about how to murder many people.

If they could use civilian jetliners today, what was to stop them using other everyday peaceful machines for similarly demented purposes? The President spoke for the nation when he decided there needed to be a large military response with a target loosely related to the new enemy.

A firestorm of bombs

Operation Enduring Freedom began with a firestorm of smart bombs, a shock and awe demonstration of the allies firepower. It soon led to the downfall of the Afghan government and the occupation of the country by the conquering allied force.

That turned out to be the relatively easy part of the plan. Creating a civilian government and political society that would exert control over the jihadist forces within the country, and would project a better image of the country abroad was more difficult.

In August 2003 the task of keeping order in Afghanistan passed to a Nato force, which allowed new units to join the USA and her allies on the ground. The plan was always to offer support and training to local security forces acting for the new government, but this turned out to be difficult to deliver.

The Nato forces stayed there for many years, and had to continue fighting Al Qaeda and other violent groups who did not accept the remit and authority of the Karzai government elected in multi-party elections in 2004.

In 2015 the country was still unable to control all the insurgent and terrorist forces within it, leading to the launch of Operation Freedom Sentinel, a further attempt by Nato to assist, protect and encourage civilian national government on a democratic model.

Afghanistan brought home to sensible observers the difficulties faced by western troops trying to carry out the western remit.

Young American or British soldiers with junior officers were put into a country where they could not speak or read the language, where they had little understanding of the religions and customs, and where they needed to be super policemen and women enforcing the peace against an ill-defined enemy.

The terrorist and insurgent forces could operate from safe houses and from friendly bases within the country. They did not wear distinctive uniforms, were willing to kill at random and offered no introductory warnings within what was meant to be a peaceful civilian society.

Quite often they aimed to kill and maim by leaving mines and bombs, booby traps and sniper fire from well-concealed places.

No easy way of winning

There was no defined battlefield. The western troops could not fire indiscriminately and had to be sure who they were attacking before they fired back. Nato personnel had to operate out of heavily armed and protected camps, and seek to impose their will for peace by passing through difficult areas using armoured vehicles or foot patrols with vigilant dispositions trying to avoid traps and enemy fire.

There was no easy way of winning as the usually unseen enemies worked away at persuading or threatening local populations into co-operating with them against the national government and their foreign army support.

This and the other Middle Eastern wars led to substantial refinement of the legal base of these actions, and new heights of control from senior individuals well away from the theatre of operations.

The allies did often use air strikes to attack presumed enemy positions and weaponry. Considerable research had to go into the targets before they could be authorised. Given the technology it became possible for the US or UK defence secretary to review the intelligence and authorise the target from thousands of miles away.

Those on the ground had a duty to ensure the intelligence was up to date. Smart weapons gave some flexibility to abort or avoid disaster if it proved the target's nature had changed after the research.

The weapons could send back film of everything that happened up to impact so there could be a detailed audit of what they had hit and how successful the raid had been, assisted by further photography of the aftermath of the explosion.

All this became very necessary, as there was a growing feeling as the wars progressed that a Nato force seeking to enforce and uphold the peace should avoid so called collateral damage. It was not acceptable to kill the wrong people by mistake in the hope that they were also killing the hard core of insurgents and terrorists.

War in Iraq...

In 2003 the allies decided on the most fateful of the Middle Eastern wars, which was to have a big impact on politics on both sides of the Atlantic.

President Bush persuaded Prime Minister Blair that the UK should join the USA in an invasion of Iraq. This was two years after the Twin Towers attack, and was not directly related to the suspects for that attack in the way the Afghan invasion had been.

Mr Bush's case was twofold. He claimed the Saddam Hussein regime in that country had created weapons of mass destruction, which represented an immediate and real threat to the West. He also argued that the regime was harbouring Al Qaeda leaders who might well be planning more terror attacks like the 9/11 one.

It was true that Saddam boasted of terror weapons, though he did not make an explicit threat against western countries and did not spell out exactly what he had the power to do if he turned hostile.

Mr Blair was nervous about the commitment he made to be a good ally, realising that the UK Parliament was not universally persuaded of the case. In particular the Labour left and the Liberal Democrats were suspicious of the claims of the governments, and the Foreign Secretary Robin Cook decided to resign in protest over the policy.

There were divisions within the Conservatives too. Some of us had misgivings about the arguments put, and some voted against despite the strong belief of the then Conservative leader that the USA was right and the intelligence must back up the claims.

Parliament duly voted for the war thanks to the cross-party support to a divided Labour party, but only after raising questions about the accuracy and nature of the intelligence concerning weapons of mass destruction.

Parliament also queried the legal base for the action, wanting the UK to obtain an explicit mandate from the UN to give it international backing. The legal advice that was released did not reassure the critics of the war, and as events unfolded the basis for assuming Iraq had weapons of mass destruction that could be deployed rapidly and dangerously against the USA and the UK wafted away.

As with the Afghan invasion the allies made rapid progress in invading the country, and soon got rid of Saddam Hussein.

In 2005 multi-party elections established the Al Maliki government in office where they stayed until 2014. There was less of a problem enforcing the law and co-operating with the civilian power than in Afghanistan, but much more of a problem justifying the action.

The invasion did not find the stockpiles of weapons of mass destruction that the statements of Mr Blair and President Bush had implied were there. It was also difficult finding the dangerous Al Qaeda leaders the regime was meant to be protecting.

Whilst many in the West appreciated another military job well done and were satisfied that a nasty dictator had been taken down, many others were concerned about the legal case for intervention and the consequences for the attitudes and determination of insurgent militant forces throughout the region.

The UK commissioned various enquiries into what had happened and allowed a full public debate about the wisdom and results of the action.

The Chilcot Inquiry did not make good reading for the government when it finally published an exhaustive report into what had happened. It illustrated the difficulties with the legal base and with the interpretation of the intelligence about the armoury and intentions of the Saddam regime.

Iraq made it much more difficult for a UK government to recommend similar military interventions again, and intensified the work on smart weapons, on use of weapons audit, and on precise control from the centre of more of the military decisions that could result in deaths.

...and then in Libya and Syria

Prime Minister Cameron's decision with France as an ally to topple the regime in Libya was another example of a military intervention that stretched public support to the limits and led to much questioning of why it had been carried out and how it made things better.

Removing the dictator once again proved a relatively easy task for the military prowess of the allies, but building a strong democratic Libya to replace the authoritarian system that was brought down proved impossible.

Libya broke up into warring factions, with considerable damage to her economy as trade and work were interrupted by the petty violence of the warring bands seeking to control parts of the country. Different cities and regions fell under different control, with continuous and debilitating violence undermining civilian work and commerce.

When it came to the possibility of intervening in Syria against the dictator Assad the UK Parliament had had enough of these wars.

Enough Conservatives threatened to vote with Labour against the war so the motion had to be remodelled to avoid asking for permission to enter hostilities, and was still lost.

By this time the long experience of what happened after a dictator was toppled played on more MPs minds. The Syrian conflict showed off the enormous complexities of these middle Eastern civil wars and made many of us ask whose side if any was the UK on?

In Syria the government started by wishing to end the regime of Assad. A good case could be made against his barbarism towards some of the people of his country, as he ruthlessly tried to put down a large and complex rebellion against his rule by a range of different forces.

Here was a man who would allow bombing of residential suburbs and of hospitals, whose ambition to recapture territory lost to his authority allowed him to kill many of the people and destroy most of the buildings in areas where there were rebel forces intermingled with non-combatants. He would also use some chemical weapons which are banned internationally. Mr Cameron tried to make that case.

Unfortunately the main opposing force to Assad was none other than Isil, who had taken over from Al Qaeda as the main terrorist anti-western group.

They were prepared to grab Middle Eastern territory at the same time as running asymmetric warfare attacks on western cities.

Many MPs argued we had no wish to assist them by helping topple Assad and create a bigger power vacuum in a destabilised Syria which they could expand to fill.

Labour looked as if they would allow the vote to go through but changed their minds on the day, leading to Mr Cameron's defeat. Parliament was closer to the national mood than the Prime Minister. A relieved nation took the view that he had missed making the dire situation in Syria worse, and avoided putting our troops in harm's way in a situation where they would find it difficult to identify and engage the enemy.

The Syrian civil war was far more complex than a simple battle between the Assad regime forces and challengers led by Isil.

Russia intervenes

To the north Kurds were trying to carve out a separate Kurdish state in the border regions near Turkey, whilst Turkey was trying to stop them. This placed a Nato ally into a position where it had more sympathy with Assad and his ally, Russia, as they too wished to defeat the Kurds. There are forces from the so-called Syrian opposition and various extreme groups.

The whole is overlaid by the battle between the Sunni groups and the Shia groups, with the former looking more to Saudi Arabia and the latter to Iran.

Russia's intervention in the conflict occurred when President Putin saw the indecision and difficulty facing the Nato allies over how to intervene and who to support.

Putin took the straightforward course of backing the Syrian government, helping them to combat Isil and many other forces seeking to damage the regime and split up the country including local allies of Nato.

So far the one good thing has been the degree of co-operation behind the scenes between Russia and Nato to avoid military clashes between their forces. In practice now Nato has to advise on any bombing mission it wishes to undertake with Russia as Russia is close to controlling the skies over the country with its ally Assad.

The UK government spent time trying to persuade MPs to vote for intervention by claiming there was a moderate opposition to Assad that we needed to assist militarily.

They wanted us to believe that the so-called moderates could raise a credible army, fight against the regime successfully and see off the violent and radical forces of opposition to Assad at the same time.

There never seemed to be enough moderates, nor did it seem likely moderates could win a war characterised by immoderate and extremely violent behaviour by the main participants on both sides. It was difficult to see how a moderate centre could emerge victorious with enough people and sufficient functioning infrastructure left for there to be any kind of life for the people who had stayed despite the brutality.

Those whom the government brought to London to represent the moderates did not present a credible case. Many people and their MPs were left thinking we did not favour either the Assad regime or Isil, which made it especially difficult to decide how to intervene. The UK government ended up effectively changing sides, as it went from wishing to topple Assad with moderate support, to wanting to attack Isil, arguably helping Assad against his worst enemies.

Avoiding Yemen

The UK has not sought to intervene in the Yemeni civil war, which is equally brutal and complex. The main conflict is said to be between the government and the Houthi rebels.

Saudi Arabia lines up with the government, and Iran with the insurgents. Again there is a strong Sunni versus Shia element to the fight. The position is complicated by various local warlords, and by the presence of Al Qaeda and Isil forces seeking territory and control over settled populations.

The Yemeni government has been on the defensive. It has lost control of the capital city to the Houthi and now has to operate out of Aden. The Houthis are able to launch missile attacks against Saudi Arabia which retaliates with aerial assaults of its own.

It is another one of the Middle Eastern complex wars where there is no obvious side to want to help, and where assisting create a peace will be difficult. The USA is having another go at trying to organise talks by applying diplomatic pressure on Saudi as one of the principal external actors.

The populists by and large are against these military interventions.

One of the least commented on differences between HIllary Clinton for the establishment and Donald Trump for the challengers was his wish to withdraw US troops from Iraq and Afghanistan and desist from further major military commitments.

In office Mr Trump is trying to get a reluctant Pentagon and State Department to carry through his wishes to bring US troops back home.

He asks what does winning look like in these interminable Middle Eastern wars? How are US interests furthered if Assad runs Syria or someone else? How can you impose democracy by bombing from 20,000 feet above the territory concerned? How does a US-led invasion lead to successful democratic politics?

The elite reply that the US and Nato are forces for good. Sometimes they do need to be deployed to remove an evil regime, and then to back the construction of a better constitution with elections and a democratic government. There has, they argue, been some success with that in both Afghanistan and Iraq.

Mr Trump has wished to see Isil defeated by anyone operating where they seek to seize power. Limited US force has been deployed in Syria against ISIL targets from the air, offering modest assistance to Russia and Assad as they go about their task of re-establishing control for the Assad-led government. Even this concerns many populist voters, who feel there are quite enough soldiers and weapons in the Middle East without Nato or the US committing forces to kill more people.

***

The USA after 9/11 set up the Guantanamo Bay prison camp to detain and interrogate suspected terrorists. This became a major flare point between the military establishment and its critics.

President Bush took the view that the USA was at war with these terrorists. They could be detained as prisoners of war, and subjected to aggressive interview to gain intelligence about terrorist networks, past abuses and possible future targets.

Critics pointed out that war is declared between established states. These people were terrorist suspects and should be treated accordingly. They should be told of the charges against them and cases presented to a court of law to try them.

If there was insufficient evidence to bring a case they should be let go. After all, the establishment kept saying it was upholding the international rules based system. Isn't innocent until proved guilty, and the right to know the charges and to put your defence fundamental to that system of international law and moral duty?

Mr Obama campaigned as candidate to close Guantanamo Bay, appreciating the case against the way the USA was handling these individuals.

Once in office he failed to carry through his promise. The establishment kept warning him that these people could be dangerous and it was best to detain them indefinitely without trial.

Congress also helped block him when he wished to transfer some of them to a jail in the USA. At one point Guantanamo housed 780 people. President Bush released 532 without trial after detention. President Obama released another 197.

Critics think this is a stain on US democracy that so many people were detained for long periods only to be allowed out with insufficient evidence even to bring them to trial. Defenders of the establishment say the world was a safer place whilst they were detained as some of them might have undertaken terrorist activities if they had not attracted the attention of the US authorities.

The West has had a bruising time in the Middle East since 9/11, though not nearly as bruising as the dreadful experiences of the peace-loving publics of Iraq, Afghanistan. Syria, Libya and Yemen as the bitter wars have gone on and on.

Populists have mainly wanted the West to cease military interference, and have been downbeat about what has been achieved. Most praise the bravery and skill of Nato's forces, but feel they were not committed in a good cause or were not committed as part of a winning political and diplomatic strategy.

The public was largely with the first interventions in the wake of the 9/11 massacre, but grew increasingly impatient and weary of the process as the wars ground on and as the complexities of the civil wars became clearer to some western commentators.

Migration fuelled

The wars themselves fuelled more migration as millions of displaced people thought they could enjoy a better life in the West than in the Middle East, which intensified the radical populist movements both sides of the Atlantic.

The moral authority of the West took a knock when the arguments about weapons of mass destruction and the legal base for the Iraq war dragged on as an important part of the national dialogue in the USA, the UK and elsewhere.

The ever looming presence of Guantanamo was a reminder that the West was compromising its values of liberty and freedom under the law to try to tackle these asymmetric warriors that threatened it. Those who truly believed in civil liberties and the rule of law thought the West should not compromise its values, even if this made tackling terrorism more difficult.

Others close to government on this occasion did wish to modify their claimed belief in a rules-based system as they argued the terrorist menace was so big it justified detention without trial or even forms of torture to try to get intelligence out of bad people.

As the arguments continued more and more populists started to disbelieve the governments who told them terrorism was a unique and huge threat which required unusual methods and military responses.

Populists started to say we do not believe you when presented with more government claims of weapons of mass destruction or immediate major threats to western society. They also came to question more and more whether the pattern of interventions made the position better or whether it might even be making it worse.

The public in Europe and America turned to the idea of keeping more people out of our countries who might prove to be jihadists, at a time when the establishments were too keen to allow in more refugees from the wars they were involved with. The populists and the establishment had a fundamental disagreement about how best to keep America and Europe safe.

Chapter 10

Large companies can lose it with their populist customers

The more the corporates act as supports and megaphones for the preoccupations of governments, the more they suffer the same dislocation from their customers

The governing elite feel comfortable in the company of big business.

Much of what they do is done in the name of helping big business. They rub along together, staying in the same hotels, attending the same international conferences and worrying about the same global problems.

Much of the big business corporate agenda is handed down from big government or derived from international treaties and summits. They flit together from Davos to a climate-change conference, whilst the same preoccupations dominate the agenda for an EU or G7 or a G20 meeting.

Just as the political elite are finding their agenda is turning voters off and causing them to prefer rival radical populist parties, so large global companies are discovering the public do not like some of their essays in public policy.

They do not share their agendas over climate change, austerity and the defence of the status quo or the so-called rules-based system. It means that whilst the populists will still buy products and services from companies whose agenda and corporate conduct they criticise, they are ever ready to look for an alternative.

In the age of the digital revolution the dislike of features of large corporate behaviour acts as a further stimulus to change, as people are ready and willing to try the new and switch supplier.

Large companies and big established government not only share the same prejudices. They share the same arrogance. They assume they are here for the long term. They can mistake the trappings of power for actual power, and assume their power will survive however they exercise it.

A government with a good majority often feels it can do unpopular things because the electorate will realise they cannot seriously vote for these no hoper challengers that do not understand the realities of power.

Ceasing to please

Power they say means making compromises and taking hard decisions. Many of the parties that have held this view are now also rans, not wanted by electorates tired of their arrogance and tired of their U-turns and broken pledges.

The same can also happen to large corporations that cease to please. In the age of social media companies are particularly vulnerable to changes of fashion and perception about them.

In an earlier period, Gerald Ratner found out that one badly expressed joke could do huge damage to his jewellery business. BP discovered that making a bad mistake with its contractors on a single well threatened the very life of the huge corporation for a while, as massive sums had to be paid to clean up and provide compensation to an angry public and host country.

Volkswagen discovered that being clever with regulations designed to cut harmful emissions was a very stupid decision which damaged its reputation badly.

The large corporation benefits from economies of scale. The costs of product development or marketing, of responding to regulation or employing the best experts can all be spread over many more customers and sales when a group has worldwide reach and decent market share.

The large corporation is also the best means yet devised of squandering the economies of scale. As the group grows, so it recruits more overhead, increases pay and perks of its senior people and gets involved in politics and society in ways that no smaller company would dream of doing.

When a group has a public affairs department, a large personnel department, a regulatory and legal department, a chief executive's department, a strategy department, a planning department and the rest it is well on the road to absorbing and spending many of the economies of scale production on itself, and well on the way to being one of those large global corporates that expresses a view and intervenes in the political life of the countries where it operates.

It is easy to forecast how it will then behave.

It will welcome a global corporate citizen and promote the establishment agenda, speaking out for more mobility of labour, more multicultural countries, more merging of national identities. It will embrace global warming as the biggest challenge facing the world, and wish to be seen to be saying the right things about it before the senior executives get into the private jet to go to another international gathering.

It will support World Bank and IMF initiatives, defend austerity policies as necessary financial discipline, but enter a caveat were they to require higher corporation tax rates. It will defend the current level and style of regulation, though it may be against some particular new measure which has a direct bearing on its own business.

This typical agenda makes the big business very remote from the concerns and views of populist voters. It makes them very suspicious of the motives and wisdom of those who say they run these large groups.

There is little buy in to the idea that corporate executives or bureaucrats deserve the multi million pound salaries they and their consultants and non-executive directors vote themselves. There is some scepticism about what some of these people actually do to make a difference to the huge organisations they live off. The agenda produces some strange paradoxes when examining corporate policy against corporate views on public policy.

The case of the oil industry

If we take the case of the oil industry in the UK we can see an extraordinary political gaucheness.

The main concern most motorists have about petrol and diesel supply is the price.

By and large motorists think the oil companies do a good job in keeping a large number of filling stations supplied with fuel, so availability is not an issue. Quality seems fine as engines thrive on what is provided.

The problem is the bill, which takes a big chunk of the wage packet for anyone using several litres a day to get to work or school or the shops.

The UK price is predominantly tax. More than 60% of the pump price goes to the UK government, and there are also taxes on the price of the raw material as well. When the world market price of oil comes down the public is angry that there has not been a similar fall in the pump price. Often it is because the tax does not go down by the same amount as the oil price.

With all their PR advisers, marketing skill and public policy advice, no oil company dares put on the pump how much is tax and how much is paid to the oil company.

Nor do they advertise to say they are busily collecting billions of pounds for the NHS by collecting high fuel taxes every time they sell some diesel or petrol. They prefer to stay unpopular and are assumed to be voracious profit takers when the main money taker is the government.

Instead the oil companies agonise over their role in global warming, and seek to reinvent themselves as green companies. They do this defensively as the strongly political greens have an agenda to end the role of the petrol and diesel vehicle as soon as possible.

No good works or warm words by oil companies will change this ambition. Meanwhile populist motorists see this green screen from oil companies as best an irrelevance and at worst a misleading diversion from supplying them with cheap fuel.

The car as battlefield

The motor car is part of the battle between populists and the establishment.

To many voters the car is an important part of their lives. It is transformational giving people freedom to get to work, to leisure activities, to visit friends, shops and much else in ways they cannot do easily or at all by public transport.

City-dwelling establishment figures often seem to ignore the importance of the car to rural and suburban dwellers who do not have access to a regular mass transit or regular bus services near their homes.

They have other options thanks to high salaries and city services ranging from chauffeured cars and taxis through the tube to pedestrian and cycle access to nearby facilities that other parts of the country can only marvel at.

The elite's policies seem to want to make cars prohibitively expensive through higher taxes on buying vehicles and high taxes on fuel, along with increasing numbers of bans and restrictions on their use. The car producers have not been good advocates of the motorists, as they too have been sucked into the corporate world of anti-car policies and pious statements.

In the UK many of the personal buyers of new cars are older people who have paid off their mortgages and seen their children depart for their separate homes.

This group often are fiercely patriotic and in favour of Brexit. They have had to listen as big car makers have been used by the UK government to argue that Brexit will be deeply damaging to their businesses because it will be unable to handle their sophisticated just-in-time assembly systems.

This has caused annoyance amongst pro-Brexit voters, who cannot see how Brexit can disrupt just-in-time systems. These systems today handle substantial numbers of components that come in from outside the EU anyway, without any apparent problems caused by tariffs and other friction at the border.

If all came in with the UK outside the EU there is no obvious reason why they should be delayed. The UK authorities can import them using authorised economic operators, pre clearance and electronic manifests as they do prior to exit from the EU.

There are good logistics companies who can do the electronic paperwork and move the lorries for exporters if they wish. Were the UK authorities to put in extra checks at ports – which they are not proposing – the car assemblers would just tell their suppliers to allow for that when deciding when to send the truck.

Current just-in-time supply has to grapple with ferry delays, road congestion and the other causes of longer journey times. It has been a curious episode when leading companies making things people like to buy have decided to disagree so strongly with a large part of their market on a political issue. It widens the gap between the corporates and the voting public.

The car industry is a good example of an industry in rapid transition thanks to social and technological change. There is the top-down attack from governments. Ironically the very global warming theory the car industry now believes in is being used to force through technical changes to car design.

First there was a big shift to diesels and now a big shift away from diesels, putting substantial investment and cost on the industry as it tries to keep up with the latest regulatory fashions.

Jaguar Land Rover in the UK, which frets about the possible impact of Brexit on its business, needs to worry more about the huge impact the switch away from diesels is having.

The company successfully transitioned many of their cars and customers onto diesels from petrol vehicles in pursuit of lower carbon dioxide emissions from greater fuel economy.

The latest fashion is for electric cars, where the conventional industry struggles to produce batteries with the range and power needed, and faces challenger companies more committed to the new engineering that electric propulsion requires. There are concerns about how green all this will prove to be given the substances used in battery manufacture, the problems with battery disposal and the reliance on fossil fuels for generating quite a lot of the electricity used to re charge them

Another battleground

There is an additional consumer attack coming from a new generation of city dwellers who think it might be better to simply hire a car with or without a driver when they need one rather than owning, maintaining and taxing one all the time.

If this catches on in a big way it means far fewer new cars will be needed as car utilisation rates will soar from the very low level achieved through ownership.

A typical UK car today is only driven for the equivalent of 11 days of the year and spends the other 355 days parked. A hire car would probably be working for ten or fifteen times as long as an owned car, meaning a huge reduction in the numbers of cars needed if many people switched to the hire-in model.

There are already businesses renting out an individual's own car to others when, for example, it is parked at an airport to generate the owner an income. The possible move to the fully automatic car that drives you around should prove very popular once the technology is tried and tested and the law codes allow the blame for accidents to attach to the equipment rather than the car occupant.

The industry is going to need plenty of friends and new customers to survive these shocks and large changes. It needs to watch out for the technology companies who are keen to develop their own fully automatic cars and may have a very different view of what a car looks like and how it should perform.

Plunging into politics in ways designed to annoy the populists out there is not a good idea, and adds to distrust of traditional companies and brands.

Bankers in trouble

The banking sector led the further loss of confidence in large corporates for its conduct during the banking crash.

The central banks and governments were good at pinning the blame almost entirely on the commercial banks for the accidents and mistakes of policy which involved them as well.

The public came to believe that the main banks had deliberately stoked up a credit bubble by advancing money to people and companies who could not afford it, and by investing and selling a range of derivative and option products said to be risk reducing which appeared in retrospect to be more self-serving.

Companies sold interest rate or exchange rate protection found they could be on the wrong end of a large bet with an investment bank. As interest rates fell for example they had to pay more for insurance against rising rates they did not need.

The bankers compounded the bad opinions by seeking to make money out of sorting out the mess and by infringing a growing number of rules the regulators set up in response to the mood that something needed to be done to control them.

There was particular annoyance in the UK and elsewhere about the need for bail outs. These large rich institutions that paid some of their employees fabulously large salaries and bonuses ended up needing public cash to prop up their capital.

The view spread widely that the banks were not behaving in a capitalist manner, accepting losses when they got it wrong. Instead the state bailed them out, allowing the executives to retain their past bonuses for writing business that turned out to be bad, and allowing the shareholders to keep some value in their shares when in practice their bank was close to bankruptcy.

I advocated making the shareholders and bondholders take more of the hit for the losses, with rapid recapitalisations and assets sales to keep the essential core going and to avoid depositor loss.

Instead a governing establishment that perversely created the conditions that brought the banks low then offered them government money to keep them going. The prospective rules for any future crisis do include living wills for the larger commercial banks.

Under these in a future crisis the shareholders and bondholders will indeed have to take the strain of paying for the losses and mistakes, with just the essential core being kept going to allow money settlement and avoid depositor loss.

The banks were unable to help themselves much by showing a willingness to lend to assist getting us out of the great recession, as the new stringent rules on cash and capital militated against them being able to support many new ventures or extra purchases.

A range of shadow banks and other institutions came into the market to advance money against property development or finance new businesses, usually at higher rates with more of an equity participation than the banks used to demand.

Banks still not close to people's hearts....

The main banks are still not close to people's hearts and have a lot of work to do to win back popular support. They are seeking to move their customers on to online banking, which is liked by some but disliked by others.

There is a sceptical group who fear online banking will be more subject to scams and fraud. A series of crimes against banks, coupled with technology errors by banks has confirmed some in their view that online accounts can be particularly dangerous.

Banks are in the front line of modern cyber wars. Their public will be unforgiving if they lose too many skirmishes against the bots, hackers and phishers.

In the new age of web banking we have seen people denied access to their money and unable to settle their bills because the bank computer has been subject to a denial of service attack.

It is becoming more and more imperative to have clear safe identifiers of who is operating an account, which in turn creates new barriers for honest people trying to access their own money.

There is also more scope in this fast-changing world for digital companies to steal a march on traditional banks by developing apps and services which the tech enthusiasts like more.

The increasing use of banks to tackle crime is also slowing down providing good service to some customers.

As many crimes involve the spending or gaining of money banks have a role in locating the proceeds of crime or the financing of crime. The increasing imposition of demands on banks to act as police means many more checks, delays and refusals of service.

Banks often now err of the side of caution and make business difficult for the law abiding as they strive to show they will be tough on crime. It is often easier in complex cases for the banks to refuse the customer an account.

...but the public still likes retail

The sector at the most visible face of the digital revolution has not lost public sympathy in the way the banks and oil companies and some car companies have.

Retail groups usually maintain more public affection, with many liking the idea of the shops and hoping they survive on the High Street.

Most retailers have also been more careful than the car companies over their political involvement, recognising more clearly that they sell a lot to populists as well as to establishment supporters.

The problem the store groups face is changing consumer behaviour. More and more people want to buy more and more things online.

Amazon and the other leading on line retailers have taken great lumps out of the market share of the traditional store groups and look likely to take more. Most traditional retailers have set up successful online versions of themselves, recognising they need to move with the consumer mood. This means double costs, with all the continuing costs of a large store chain and the costs of an online competitor to it. The new discount online retailers still have a substantial cost edge when they reach a certain level of volume.

Retailers lose the public mood when they get too tricksy with discounts and promotions, or when they are thought to be offering exploitative prices. The high level of store and online competition means on the whole pricing is honest and competitive. They can also lose public support if their boss is seen to be taking too much money out of the business or undertakes deals which attract the wrong kind of press and regulatory attention.

The large internet businesses have until recently wowed the public with their products and services.

An increasing share of the consumer spend goes on smart phones, film downloads, broadband and tablets. Large revenues are now generated by the substantial advertising undertaken on social media. The public particularly liked the free-at-the-point-of-use features of many internet services from Google to Facebook.

More recently there have been issues raised about the nature and scale of the advertising revenues raised by these companies to support their services.

In some cases doubt has been cast over the ethics of the use made of the information people have willingly supplied to internet-based service providers, when it is sold on or exploited commercially. There have also been scandals about data loss or theft compromising the online security of users.

If someone has features of their identity stolen from a social media site it might make it easier for a cyber criminal to get into that person's bank account or credit card and steal from them. Gradually as they grow and become very profitable the large internet corporates will be placed under more regulation and expected to pay more tax. Their images will lose lustre as they come to share more of the characteristics and foibles of older large corporations.

Corporate greed is disliked

Corporate greed remains an unattractive feature of some businesses with the public disliking multi-million pound remuneration packages, and disliking incentive schemes which encourage actions against the interests of the customers.

Banks were thought to have missold too many products because commission or bonus was paid to those doing the selling.

The public makes a clear distinction between the pay of an entrepreneur and the pay of a senior executive of a large established business.

If someone owns a business which is very successful most have no problems if that boss wishes to take large sums out of the profits for his own use. They judge the business on what it offers and what prices it charges and do not get jealous about the owner creator making a lot of money himself.

They are more sceptical about how much hired-in bosses of large companies do to improve the business and serve the customers.

Large businesses can get a mauling in the press for high pay and big pay rises, and for bonus schemes which are too easy or rigged against the shareholders. They can also these days face substantial votes against their remuneration policy from institutional shareholders seeking to catch the public mood and represent the many who collectively own these companies through their pension funds and insurance funds.

The payment of company and executive tax is also a flare point between some large companies and the wider audience of consumers and electors.

Profit-maximising companies retain expensive lawyers and tax experts to seek to minimise their tax bills by staying within the law but understanding its opportunities to lower the effective tax charge.

Governments are becoming increasingly hostile to tax avoidance, which is legal, and making it more like tax evasion, which is illegal. Public opinion too is broadly hostile to successful tax reduction by large companies. People are more understanding of the way their neighbours may pay cash to a small tradesman who does not declare all his income, or may themselves hire a small business to do a job to be below the VAT threshold to make the work cheaper.

As in any era there is a fair share of corporate scandals when individual chairmen or chief executives are caught out breaking the rules of the company or offending people's view of good conduct or even breaking the law.

The recent disclosures by Volkswagen over exhausts, by Nissan over executive pay and perks and by Sports Direct over corporate governance add fuel to the populist fire that big businesses are all the same and it is controlled by an elite distanced from the customers.

In the worst cases senior executives are found guilty of criminal acts. It is all part of the same story line of the populists.

Just as they increasingly say they do not believe governments, they don't believe a good many companies either. The more the corporates act as supports and megaphones for the preoccupations of governments, the more they suffer the same dislocation from the voters and consumers. The more they look after themselves before their customers, the more critical people become.

Chapter 11

The elite and the thought police

The advent of citizen's media poses new problems for the authorities

One of the worst features of the modern public conversation is the bad language, vitriol and personal abuse that pours forth in social media masquerading as democratic debate.

Anyone who ventures a view, holds public office or sets out the details of their life online becomes immediate public property, subject to abuse and to condemnation often by anonymous bloggers and tweeters.

The traditional media complains that they are not allowed to hurl libel and abuse in the way some users of the social media do. They worry about how to compete.

To keep attention away from the challengers, they often become more extreme in the way they treat interview guests. They have a passion to set people up, confront them with lies and half-truths and evoke extreme responses from people put under pressure.

The noise of the social media encourages the worse traits of conventional media competing for audience. They pander to a gallery of listeners and viewers thought to have short attention spans and liking extreme language and emotional reactions. The public conversation gets coarser with more violent or aggressive language.

The diatribes and false allegations come from all sides.

Some come from the establishment themselves who use these same tactics and techniques to stifle debate they do not like. They sometimes seek to sully people speaking out well against their ideas and actions.

In the USA it is now par for the course that both Democrats and Republicans think it a standard part of politics to seek to bring down the president of the other persuasion. They try to open impeachment proceedings for alleged infringements of criminal law.

The left in the UK specialises in unpleasant personal attacks and campaigns to try to upend their opponents. The anti-migrant right in many places wants to use disobliging language about recent arrivals that creates more tensions within mixed communities. In the UK the modern Labour party is wrestling with alleged anti-Jewish feelings and statements from senior people in the party.

Part of the pressure which forms the populist parties comes from a sense of frustration about what people think they are allowed to say.

Whilst to some the tone and tenor of debate on the conventional media can seem brutish, to others it is still circumscribed by laws of libel and the praiseworthy wish to avoid hate speech.

Populist voters are likely to be driven to social media and websites with compatible views to theirs by disliking the consensus view. They may object to the relative restraint that dominates much of the official conversation and the output of the conventional media. They are also driven to social media because they hope to be allowed to say things that are actually forbidden or they think are forbidden elsewhere.

The exchange of sceptical views on climate change takes place largely this way because people will be called climate change deniers and ridiculed or scolded by the establishment media. Alternative views to the economic orthodoxy, whether of the socialist or free market wings, are also more likely to find the oxygen of publicity outside the main media.

Where freer speech is needed

The most sensitive area where freer speech is sought is over issues of race, religion, ethnicity and migration.

The UK and other advanced countries have introduced substantial law codes to outlaw hate speech and to ban or discourage discussion which questions toleration, multicultural solutions and a generous spirit towards refugees and asylum seekers.

These laws have been well considered by the establishment, keen to seek understanding and mutual respect in mixed communities. Some populists see this as deliberately closing down debate on an issue which matters to them. They seek ways to have a legitimate debate about numbers, about the relative treatment of new migrants and settled people, about how to treat criminals from foreign countries and how far we should go in requiring assimilation.

Some wish to go much further. They want to argue about racial and religious characteristics of differing groups, wish to assert there are group characteristics in some cases which they do not like, and want to argue that anyone coming to live in a country should learn its language and customs and mirror the lifestyles of the majority.

A redefinition of crime

I have no wish to give more prominence to these arguments nor to spell them out in detail with specifics. On this I agree with the establishment that language which incites hatred should be banned, and that considering groups of people to have undesirable or non-compliant characteristics, attitudes or actions because of their racial or religious background is untrue and unacceptable.

That will upset some of the populists reading this, who will say that proves their point. There is a conspiracy to stop them talking about things that matter to them.

The tensions flare up particularly about crimes committed by people recently arrived in the country from overseas places and cultures, as we saw in Germany.

The establishment points out that criminals come from all backgrounds. Most migrants from any given country or religious background are not criminals and it is wrong to tag them with the bad reputation earned by a few.

Some populists protest that in their view certain groups commit more crimes than others, and argue that sometimes the background culture seems to them to encourage certain unacceptable behaviours. They feel they are prevented from making much of this by laws designed to prevent hate speech and to prevent individual groups being targeted for blame or social isolation. Their wish to make certain claims can by definition be racist or an attempt to discriminate against people because of their backgrounds and religions.

It is true there is a more extensive thought police in the UK and the EU today than 30 years ago.

We are seeing a redefinition of crime. Casual theft and burglary were once the bread and butter crimes of the UK police. Murder was mercifully rare and rightly attracted high level and substantial police attention to find the criminal. Today more emphasis goes on crimes on social media, on fraud often perpetrated through digital devices and on abuse said in person.

There has been a spate of enquiries into long ago crime and even crimes committed by people now dead, to make amends for the inadequacies of past crime detection and prosecution.

This has made some populists claim that modern governments are not trying to deal with real crime as they see it.

The establishment replies that if someone has been watching porn on their computer or smart phone, they are indirectly abusing the person recording the item. Such conduct may also lead on to physical abuse of others in person.

If someone is busy joining in social media conversations abusing various racial and ethnic groups they may then turn up at a rally or join a gang which carries through physical attacks upon those same abused groups. Criminals using computers make detection easier.

Using a computer in certain ways is now a crime in itself. If someone downloads bomb making, training kits for terrorism or pornographic images of children they are committing offences, which should be crimes in anyone's book.

Growing frustrations

The populists still feel frustrated even when the logic of escalation from computer to real events is explained and when the authorities show they understand often the computer is a device used to allow a further or future crime.

The frustration over migration policy leads to a frustration about the limits placed on talking about it. The strong disagreement with climate change policy leads to impatience with attempts to close the debate down.

The tensions are highest over terrorism. Many populists feel that western governments use fear of terrorism to excess to allow them to censor and control thoughts more than they should and to justify wars and interventions which many think unwise.

There is no doubt that terrorist themselves have taken to social media and to computer hacking to try to create havoc and further their aims, so the state does need to take some action to intercept their messages and help safeguard systems.

The dilemma is acute for all of us.

Many populists both think the state should censor and control them less, but think the state should be more vigilant and tougher on those they dislike who do disrupt the state and the lives of others.

The person who struggles to remember and use all the codes to get into their bank account and who is confronted with yet more anti money laundering questions and checks when they wish to spend some of their own legitimate taxed income can be forgiven for thinking there is too much regulatory and government control over them.

If that same person then suffers from a computer scam where someone removes money from their account by false pretences or by inserting malware into the system that same person demands to know why the bank and government had not done more to protect their money.

The actions of the Russian and Chinese states show how modern powerful computers and social media can be used to manipulate public opinion, and can be deployed as attack vehicles against perceived international enemies.

The West wants a more open approach with more freedoms for individuals to use these great new technologies without the state checking up on them or trying to manipulate their opinions.

We are now in a world where there are so many cameras around people feel spied on the whole time.

Those of us who aim to keep the law can say what is the problem as if you are doing nothing wrong you have nothing to fear. Others say they still like some privacy and are not happy with the state knowing where they are, how they travelled there, what they have spent money on recently and all the rest of the data which the new systems collect and could be made to divulge.

If you travel with a smart phone on you can be traced. If you travel on the tube with an Oystercard your every journey and its timings are logged. If you walk the streets you will be on camera in many places. If you travel by motorway you will be filmed.

All the money you put through your bank account is held as data by your bank. Your smartphone knows a lot about your life and remembers more than you do. Many of these things bring us greater convenience, but in the wrong hands this data could be used against you. Any divergence between the story you tell others about your lifestyle and movements and what you actually do can now be exposed and proven.

So far the West has tried to give more rights to individuals to ensure their data is held safely. It has given more duties to large companies and governments to only hold that data they must hold, only to use what they need to use, and not to share with people other than those who need access to it to serve you. It does not always work out like that.

Governments want our data

Government increasingly wants to use the data for enforcement from speeding to tax. The very expensive and complicated General Data Protection Regulation of the EU, faithfully transposed into UK law, makes a new industry out of data compliance and makes innovative use of data more difficult for EU based companies.

The wish to prevent terrorists, sex abusers and other nasty criminals using the web and social media is leading to more censorship and regulation of what was once semi-private space. Some of the law abiding feel they are made to comply too much and too often and want to see better targeting of effort.

There is a battle about how far the state should go in imposing the same standards that apply to the conventional media onto social media where the public themselves acts as editors and content providers. That is a difficult judgement.

There is then another battle over how far the state should go in laying down in law limits to free speech in areas like religion, culture, identity and migration.

The populists fear an establishment stitch up, using fears of terrorism and civil unrest to make unreasonable inroads into limiting debate. The establishment in the West can rightly point to a big difference between how critical people can be here about the governments, and what is allowed in China.

Chinese people do not have unlimited access to western sites, and are restricted about accessing critical comment of their country and leadership. That fortunately would still be a bridge too far for the censors of the advanced country states, much as they might like to close down sections of the debate.

The battle about censorship is an old one. The advent of citizen's media poses new problems for the authorities. They have a legitimate case to make that social media should not be a breeding ground for terrorists, fraudsters and racists.

The public has a legitimate right to resist censorship of their use of the social media just because it fails to suit the state or is at variance with the establishment view. In some cases now when the state says it needs to regulate more to stop crime, the populists reply "We don't believe you".

Why the elite is not believed

Crying wolf is no longer an option

The world changed in the advanced democracies early in this century. The traditional centre right and centre left parties that had alternated in power comfortably in the post 1945 world either had to reform their attitudes or they lost their grip on power.

New challenger parties emerged that could overthrow the ancient regimes in a single election, as Syriza did in Greece and En Marche did in France.

In the UK the Conservatives had to adopt Brexit as its own to reunite the forces of conservatism. In the USA it took the unconventional Donald Trump to wrestle the Republican party from its establishment personnel and attitudes into a different irreverent more radical force for change.

Two defining events contributed most to this peaceful revolution.

The pursuit of wars in the Middle East which began as wars on terror and terrorists, became a vast enduring and messy set of campaigns to topple regimes, seeking to remodel constitutions and governments in a range of Arab countries.

The war in Iraq in particular caused a backlash in both the USA and in Europe, especially in the UK. Administrations that had taken the decisions to go to war found themselves having to defend the legal basis for their actions.

They were subject to an avalanche of criticism for wars that lasted too long, killed too many people and did not have an easy outcome when it came time to rebuild.

Trying to create functioning multi-party liberal democracies in the sands of the Arabian territories proved difficult. The public back home became restless, thinking too much had been asked of the military with too little diplomatic ability to deliver the better political outcomes people wanted.

Worse still the wars displaced many people and turned hundreds of thousands into refugees, seeking a new home in Europe or the USA. This broadened the battle between the elites who favoured generous treatment and a welcome to refugees and plenty of people who wanted to impose limits on how many could come.

Large groups of voters raised objections about the impact mass migration would have on their own lifestyle, job opportunities and housing.

The banking crash of 2008-9 had an even bigger adverse impact on traditional parties and politicians.

Why hadn't the experts and the political leaders foreseen the crash? Why had they allowed so much credit to build up in the good times? Why had they presided over such an abrupt and damaging end to the credit expansion?

Living standards took several years in the USA and UK to recover above their 2007 levels. In some parts of the Eurozone they still languish beneath the levels of a decade earlier ten years later.

Disillusion grows

Understandably voters grew disillusioned with the parties and leaders who had done this to them, and looked around for new ideas and new people who might offer something better.

This pressure was most acute in the countries of the Eurozone most damaged by the economic fallout.

The architecture of the Euro added to the losses compared to the advanced countries with independent economies and free floating currencies. Greece and Cyprus got on the wrong end of disputes with the Euro authorities and went through worse banking crises than the rest.

The European Central Bank decided to discipline them by denying their commercial banks automatic access to funds in response to overruns on the public deficit or failure to improve the capital position of the commercial banks.

Depositors as well as share and bond investors in the banks were asked to help pay the bills in Cyprus with a haircut on larger deposits. Ireland and Spain took time to adjust to the property and banking crash they experienced when the credit was turned off as the banking squeeze of 2009 developed.

This left electorates feeling powerless, as all the time they and their government wanted to stay in the currency there was little their elected officials could do to cushion the blows or to alter direction of policy.

Politicians who wanted to get elected to govern discovered they needed to offer a different message from the conventional parties.

Politicians could no longer rely on a modest touch on the tiller of state and trying to appeal to a limited number of allegedly moderate voters in the middle to tip the election their way.

The new politics required noisy and loud campaigns attracting people with strong views and negative attitudes towards the establishment.

Some parties emerged who wanted to move towards a much more socialist approach than the traditional centre left had proposed. They appealed to people with very little that a bigger redistribution of income and wealth led by a strong state would help them. Large scale nationalisation and state intervention would be needed. Greedy capitalism and overpowerful multinational companies had to be tamed.

Other parties argued that too many migrants were holding down wages and limiting access to homes and public services, so numbers needed to be curbed and borders reinforced against illegal arrivals.

Large tax cuts were needed to kick start faster growth. In the Euro area parties of right and left were critical of the EU and Euro scheme, and sought ways to circumvent or break open its strict disciplines. They agreed with each other that budget deficits should be larger and an economic stimulus administered by higher spending and or lower taxes.

Tolerance and collaboration

The elite felt they were trying to hold together a precious world order, based on rules, international treaties and established consensual expertise.

They speak up for the admirable virtues of tolerance and collaboration. They believe global warming to be a major threat to civilisation and seek to take urgent action to reduce human carbon dioxide output. They see the Euro as a force for uniting Europe, and its disciplines as a necessary price for unity and good government.

They believe in international bodies from the UN to the IMF, from the World Bank to the world climate change conferences. They see the modern world as complex, in need of expert direction, interconnected and moving towards global government and direction. They see nationalism as a potentially unsettling and dangerous force.

They encourage migration of talent and ideas to dilute individual senses of identity and place. They are afraid the public do not understand all the subtleties they think they see in the world. They despair at some of the results of elections. They think Mr Trump is an unruly force that does harm, and think Brexit is a bad idea.

The elites have often adopted negative political campaigns to dismiss or crush their radical populist opponents. They communicate a scorn for the easy phrases of the frustrated and for the understandings of the new forces in politics.

Somewhat world wearily they try to explain through repetition of their honed soundbites that the world rests on the international order they keep growing. They defend austerity policies as being essential.

They can rightly point to wayward governments that have printed too much money and sought to borrow excessively who have ended up doing more damage to living standards and economic output.

The rise of the new

They argue that the western democratic nations do need to intervene militarily where autocracies become too powerful and may one day threaten the peace. They talk of grown up politics, based around the programmes of the IMF, the lending of the World Bank, the directives of the climate change conferences, the requirements of a network of international treaties, and the rules of the EU and Euro.

On the other side of the dispute a host of new parties and political movements jostle to take power and call for change.

Lega and 5 Star (Cinque Stelle) in Italy, En Marche and the National Front in France, Brexit and Corbyn's left-wing socialism in the UK, Trumpism in the USA, a new nationalism in Poland and Hungary and Vox, Podemos and Cuidadanos in Spain are all making inroads into the old system, and many of them are now in office.

There is a wish to follow national democratic agendas with less genuflection to international bodies and treaties. There is more wish to expand economies even if that means borrowing a bit more and taxing a bit less. There is a wish to limit migration. There is a reluctance to intervene militarily in the Middle East in the way Presidents Bush, Clinton and Obama did.

The public want change. They have grown tired of too many wars that do not seem to produce good political results either for the west waging them or for the countries the west is trying to help.

They want limits placed on migration to allow more economic and cultural stability in their countries. They want higher living standards and are understandably critical of the economic policies of the last decade.

In much of the Eurozone in particular the slump in real incomes over the last ten years has been desultory, testing the established political party structure to destruction.

Using social media, people can communicate their frustrations with established politics and parties to each other rapidly and often with brutal language.

Many people tire of the way the conventional media handles politics and reports on their daily lives. They see through many of the tired soundbites of conventional politics, and are cynical about what many parties say and why they say it.

The media makes it worse

The media is in a very competitive era, facing much competition from cheap or free options. It tends to go for shock-jock styles of handling issues and tackling politics, to make it more extreme in the hope that increases the size and participation of the audience. That in some ways makes it worse, adding to the frustrations of voters with some politicians and their parties.

The public is often sceptical of what is said and what passes for political debate, to the point where they simply do not believe it. They have heard too many dire warnings and false forecasts from the elite and their big global institutions to take each new threat seriously.

In the UK that was subjected to a long and bad dose of Project Fear over the EU issue the cynicism has become particularly great, as practically all the short-term forecasts about the impact of voting to leave proved way too pessimistic. Donald Trump plays on the considerable scepticism about how serious a threat global warming might be.

More voters warm to the traditional and to the more local. They find it difficult to relate to global trends and international values. They do not see themselves as citizens of the world, but as citizens of their own country, often rooted in a particular city or local area.

In the USA they could relate to Mr Trump's Put America first rhetoric. In parts of Europe they belong to nationalist movements to get their region out from under a federate national state, as in Catalonia or Padania in Italy, or to Eurosceptic movements to loosen the ties of Brussels over their country.

The elite in Europe began by encouraging stronger senses of regional identity to loosen ties to nation states, but now unites with the member nations to rein in the regional self-government forces.

The elite has many able and sensible people in it. The finest work its institutions achieve is outstanding. The most active and energetic business people, researchers, scientists and technologists have taken us to new heights of collective achievement.

In the west, despite the 2008 crash, living standards are high and advancing.

People love much of the new technology and the range of new services the digital revolution has produced.

What they are saying is that politics needs to catch up, and professionals generally need to share more with their voters, clients and patients now we are all empowered with more knowledge through the internet.

If the main political parties continue to take voters for granted and treat them as fools, good only for few project fear campaigns, we should expect more dramatic political change.

The elite will lecture the voters with their views of why we need the liberal world order, reminding us of all the good it does. The voters may bellow back "We don't believe you" even when the elite is telling the truth. If members of the elite continue to cry wolf, they may find they are out of a job.

Bite-Sized Public Affairs Books are designed to provide insights and stimulating ideas that affect us all in, for example, journalism, social policy, education, government and politics.

They are deliberately short, easy to read, and authoritative books written by people who are either on the front line or who are informed observers. They are designed to stimulate discussion, thought and innovation in all areas of public affairs. They are all firmly based on personal experience and direct involvement and engagement.

The most successful people all share an ability to focus on what really matters, keeping things simple and understandable. When we are faced with a new challenge most of us need quick guidance on what matters most, from people who have been there before and who can show us where to start. As Stephen Covey famously said, "The main thing is to keep the main thing, the main thing."

But what exactly is the main thing?

Bite-Sized books were conceived to help answer precisely that question crisply and quickly and, of course, be engaging to read, written by people who are experienced and successful in their field.

The brief? Distil the 'main things' into a book that can be read by an intelligent non-expert comfortably in around 60 minutes. Make sure the book enables the reader with specific tools, ideas and plenty of examples drawn from real life. Be a virtual mentor.

We have avoided jargon – or explained it where we have used it as a shorthand – and made few assumptions about the reader, except that they are literate and numerate, involved in understanding social policy, and that they can adapt and use what we suggest to suit their own, individual purposes. Most of all the books are focused on understanding and exploiting the changes that we witness every day but which come at us in what seems an incoherent stream.

They can be read straight through at one easy sitting and then referred to as necessary – a trusted repository of hard-won experience.

Bite-Sized Books Catalogue

Business Books

Maiqi Ma
    Win with China
        Acclimatisation for Mutual Success Doing Business with
        China
Elena Mihajloska
    Bridging the Virtual Gap
        Building Unity and Trust in Remote Teams
Rob Morley
    Agile in Business
        A Guide for Company Leadership
Gillian Perry
    Managing the People Side of Change
        Ten Short Steps to Success in IT Outsourcing
Saibal Sen
    Next Generation Service Management
        An Analytics Driven Approach
Don Sharp
    Nothing Happens Until You Sell Something
        A Personal View of Selling Techniques

Lifestyle Books

Anna Corthout
    Alive Again
        My Journey to Recovery
Phil Davies
    Don't Worry Be Happy
        A Personal Journey
Phil Davies
    Feel the Fear and Pack Anyway
        Around the World in 284 Days
Stuart Haining
    My Other Car is an Aston
        A Practical Guide to Ownership and Other Excuses to Quit
        Work and Start a Business
Bill Heine
    Cancer – Living Behind Enemy Lines Without a Map
Regina Kerschbaumer
    Yoga Coffee and a Glass of Wine
        A Yoga Journey

Gillian Perry
  Capturing the Celestial Lights
    A Practical Guide to Imagining the Northern Lights
Arthur Worrell
  A Grandfather's Story
    Arthur Worrell's War

Public Affairs Books

Eben Black
  Lies Lobbying and Lunch
    PR, Public Affairs and Political Engagement – A Guide
John Mair and Richard Keeble (Editors)
  Investigative Journalism Today:
    Speaking Truth to Power
John Mair, Richard Keeble and Farrukh Dhondy (Editors)
  V.S Naipaul:
    The legacy
Christian Wolmar
  Wolmar for London
    Creating a Grassroots Campaign in a Digital Age
John Mair and Neil Fowler (Editors)
  Do They Mean Us – Brexit Book 1
    The Foreign Correspondents' View of the British Brexit
John Mair, Alex De Ruyter and Neil Fowler (Editors)
  The Case for Brexit – Brexit Book 2
David Bailey, John Mair and Neil Fowler (Editors)
  Keeping the Wheels on the Road – Brexit Book 3
    UK Auto Post Brexit
Paul Davies, John Mair and Neil Fowler
  Will the Tory Party Ever Be the Same? – Brexit Book 4
    The Effect of Brexit
John Mair and Neil Fowler (Editors)
  Oil Dorado
    Guyana's Black Gold
Sir John Redwood
  We Don't Believe You
    Why Populists and the Establishment see the world
    differently

John Mills
>Economic Growth Post Brexit
>>How the UK should Take on the World

Fiction

Paul Davies
>The Ways We Live Now
>>Civil Service Corruption, Wilful Blindness, Commercial Fraud, and Personal Greed – a Novel of Our Times

Paul Davies
>Coming To
>>A Novel of Self-Realisation

Victor Hill
>Three Short Stories
>>Messages, The Gospel of Vic the Fish, The Theatre of Ghosts

Children's Books

Chris Reeve – illustrations by Mike Tingle
>The Dictionary Boy
>>A Salutary Tale

Fredrik Payedar
>The Spirit of Chaos
>>It Begins

Printed in Great Britain
by Amazon